DARK VICTORY

PLAY IN THREE ACTS

BY GEORGE BREWER, JR. AND BERTRAM BLOCH

★

★

DRAMATISTS
PLAY SERVICE
INC.

CAST OF CHARACTERS

(The characters listed below are in the revised version of this play, as printed in the present volume.)

DR. FREDERICK STEELE, 35 to 40, *a distinguished surgeon, with New England reserve, forceful, direct.*

MISS WAINWRIGHT, 25 to 40, *a competent office assistant and nurse.*

DR. PARSONS, *about 60, successful physician, but not a specialist.*

JUDITH TRAHERNE, 27, *pleasure-loving, sophisticated, wealthy, very attractive, and capable of deep emotion.*

ALDEN BLAINE (*woman*), 35 to 50, *smart society writer of superficial fiction.*

BILL EWING, 25 to 35,
CONNIE, *his wife,* 25 to 35, } *sophisticated, " country club " set.*
JANETTE BORDEN, 25 to 35,
LESLIE CLARKE, 25 to 35,

MISS JENNY, 60, *New England ex-school teacher.*

MICHAEL, *Irish groom, tall, determined.*

JOSIE, *maid.*

POSTMAN, *New England rural type.*

MAN, *to bring in shadow-box.*

SCENE

Living-room of Judith's Long Island home (Acts I and II); and living-room of Steele's small Vermont home (Act III).

TIME

The present.

Dark Victory was first produced by Alexander McKaig at the Plymouth Theater, New York, November 7, 1934, with the following cast:

DR. FREDERICK STEELE ....Earle Larimore
MISS WAINWRIGHT ....Mildred Wall
DR. PARSONS ....Frederick Leister
JUDITH TRAHERNE ....Tallulah Bankhead
ALDEN BLAINE ....Ann Andrews
JOSIE ....Myra Hampton
MICHAEL ....Edgar Norfolk
LESLIE CLARKE ....Dwight Fiske
MISS JENNY ....Helen Strickland
POSTMAN ....Lewis Dayton

Please note that the above is the original cast. Additional characters have been added in the revised version of the play printed in this volume. See cast of characters on page 3.

DARK VICTORY

ACT I

Living-room of JUDITH TRAHERNE'S *house on Long Island, quietly luxurious, comfortable. Doors* L., R. *and* C. *French windows* L. *of* C. *One of these must have curtains or hangings that can be drawn inward and outward, allowing sunlight to come in and be shut out. Fireplace* R. *or* L. *if practicable, but not essential. Necessary furniture includes a sofa, four or five chairs, desk or desk-like table, and two small tables. Phone on one of side tables. Grand piano placed as desired, but this may be omitted.*

DR. STEELE *is sitting on sofa reading some typewritten pages. He glances at his wrist-watch and rises.*

STEELE. Damn Parsons for getting me into this! (*Tosses pages on table. Inspects room. Picks up book and puts it down. Returns to table as* MISS WAINWRIGHT, *his secretary, appears in door* L.) Any sign of 'em?

WAIN. (*Grimly.*) No.

STEELE. Splendid! (*Takes hat and starts for door* R.) Come on.

WAIN. It's only ten-thirty, Dr. Steele.

STEELE. I have to be at Grand Central Station at one-thirty.

WAIN. But you can't walk out like this.

STEELE. Why not?

WAIN. Because you were called down here to do a job and—you haven't done it.

STEELE. I was called down here to see a dying patient and I find that she's galloped eight miles cross country to a hunt breakfast and that Dr. Parsons is chasing around the country after her in a car. . . . As far as I'm concerned, the show's over. So let's go.

WAIN. We still have an hour.

STEELE. With all this traffic? Not on your life!

5

WAIN. Have I ever let you miss a train?

STEELE. I've waited nine years for this train, Waney, and I'm not taking any chances on missing it. (*Phone rings.* WAINWRIGHT *answers.*)

WAIN. Hello—Yes, I'll wait. (*To* STEELE.) New York on the wire.

STEELE. I'm not here—if necessary, I'm dead.

WAIN. Hello—No. This is Miss Wainwright, Dr. Steele's secretary. I'm sorry, but Dr. Steele has closed his office—permanently, yes.—I'm afraid not. He's leaving for Vermont today. No, he's not coming back. You're welcome,—good-bye. (*Hangs up.*) The Neurological wanted you for an emergency operation.

STEELE. I suppose this'll keep up until I'm actually on the train.

WAIN. Probably.

STEELE. Gosh, I'm sick of it!

WAIN. I know, Dr. Steele, you're sick of it . . . tired of being the country's leading brain surgeon; you dislike being a specialist; you loathe the formality of New York, so you're going to bury yourself in a little hick town in Vermont where you can sit on the cracker-box at the general store in your shirt-sleeves and whittle! —when you're not delivering Fresh Native Vermont babies! (STEELE *laughs delightedly.*) Isn't it true?

STEELE. And it was all working out very nicely until Parsons got me into this mess. (*Picks up case history again from table, studies it.*) What does he expect me to do? Make a diagnosis offhand from this kind of a history?

WAIN. It's been known to happen before.

STEELE. He's cracked!

WAIN. He's very worried.

STEELE. Exactly what did he say?

WAIN. "Tell Dr. Steele it's a matter of life or death, that I absolutely have to have his advice."

STEELE. Then why in blazes isn't he here with his patient?

WAIN. He didn't tell her you were coming.

STEELE. (*Shrewdly.*) He's afraid of this girl, isn't he?

WAIN. My guess is he was chiefly afraid she wouldn't want to see you.

STEELE. Well, I don't want to see her, either, so let's clear out now, and we'll all be happy.

WAIN. (*Glances at wrist-watch.*) We'll give them fifteen minutes more.

STEELE. Very well, fifteen minutes. I don't want to let Parsons down, but you know, Waney, I can't be of any real help to him. You can't make a snap judgment in a case of this sort, and there's no time for —— (*Off-stage noise* L.) Maybe that's Parsons now. (WAINWRIGHT *goes out* L. *A moment later she returns shaking her head.*) What is it?

WAIN. A portable X-ray machine from the hospital.

STEELE. WHAT!

WAIN. They're setting it up in the next room. They've brought an automatic developer; solution for the wet plates; ground glass shadow box—everything.

STEELE. Well, this explains it! It's all perfectly clear now. Parsons has gone mad and invented the whole thing—poor devil has been to the movies just once too often.

WAIN. How about the set? The layout? (*Points to windows.*) The garden; the stables; the grounds?

STEELE. It's probably one of their Long Island studios —— (*Knock at door* L. *Enter* MAN *carrying shadow box.*)

MAN. Where do you want this?

WAIN. Oh—(*Indicating corner table* R.) over there.

MAN. (*Sets it up. Plugs in to outlet; snaps light on and off.*) It's O. K. (*Exit.*)

WAIN. He looked real.

STEELE. Yes.

WAIN. This must be a Goldwyn production.

STEELE. But, Waney—it's fantastic!

WAIN. Dr. Parsons knows you use X-ray as routine.

STEELE. Yes, but—well, I suppose he —— Oh, I'll be ——! (*Sits down.*)

WAIN. We still have thirteen minutes. Suppose in the interests of my sanity as well as yours that you tell me what this case is all about? (*She hands him the history.*)

STEELE. God knows. I can't make out whether Parsons has written a case history—or a novel. It seems that the glamorous lady of this manor house was injured in a fall from a horse while riding with a young man. At first Parsons thought it was a heart case—then a head injury—now he doesn't know what to think.

WAIN. That's helpful. . . . (*Goes to him.*) When was the accident? (WAINWRIGHT *sits small chair* C.)

STEELE. About three weeks ago.—Isn't this typical of Parsons?

7

(*Looks at papers.*) " Miss Judith Traherne, twenty-seven; daughter of Mrs. Robert Traherne, widow of the late wire manufacturer." Imagine putting that stuff in a case history! " Patient of good physique; excellent athlete, hard rider." He omits to say hard drinker. (*Rises.*)

WAIN. Why assume the worst? (*She rises—crosses to shadow box to glance at something on it, then back to* C.)

STEELE. I could assume lots worse. I once spent a week-end in a place like this—one week-end.

WAIN. What was the impression?

STEELE. Somehow I seem to remember a lot of—horses.

WAIN. Noble animal!

STEELE. Yes, but—the people who collect them! You couldn't stick it twenty-four hours, Waney, if you had the mentality of a sparrow.

WAIN. Sounds like just the life for a sparrow.

STEELE. In any case our heroine was suddenly thrown and Parsons was sent for. Apparently she had a fainting spell after she got home. Sprained back, badly bruised—then Parsons discovers she has an irregular heart—further on he says she's lost weight—resents being questioned. H'm, that's funny. Apparently she's suffered from headache ever since, and that's about all except Parsons thinks she's really sick.

WAIN. Not much to go by.

STEELE. No—all told (*Rises and crosses* R.) I gather she's been a difficult patient—she sounds to me like bad news.

WAIN. You won't have to bother with her.

STEELE. No. Two hours and I'll be on my way—two hours and I'll be out of this overpopulated menagerie.

WAIN. Has New York been as bad as that?

STEELE. Nine years—(*Turns to her.*) and not one sight of those hills. You don't know what they mean to me. I was born under them; lived in their shadow until the war, and I have no peace without them.

WAIN. Some people feel that way about the sea.

STEELE. Yes, the sea and the hills—the two poles of the great magnet: Earth. Waney, I have just one regret, and you know what . . . (*Suddenly door* R. *opens and* PARSONS *enters. He is immaculately dressed. His manner is brisk, sharp, and rather fussy.*)

PARSONS. Hello, Steele. (*To* WAIN.) Good morning.

WAIN. Good morning, Dr. Parsons. . . . I think I'll have a look at that X-ray machine. (*Exits* L. STEELE *and* PARSONS *size one another up.* STEELE *is ominously silent.*)

PARSONS. Now don't start being cantankerous! It's not my fault—how the devil did I know she'd take it into her head to do a thing like this! (*Challenging him directly.*) When are you leaving?

STEELE. In eleven minutes.

PARSONS. When does your train go?

STEELE. One-thirty.

PARSONS. Can't you possibly take a later one?

STEELE. No.

PARSONS. Why not?

STEELE. The later trains don't make connections.

PARSONS. Stop fiddling with those books and listen to me a minute: I'm not attempting to persuade you to give up your fool plan. I've tried everything I could on that score and failed.

STEELE. Thank God for that.

PARSONS. There's no use—you're too set in your ways—too Yankee—too stubborn and too old, but I am going to ask you a favor.

STEELE. After that? No wonder you've made a success!

PARSONS. I want you to stay over and give this girl a thorough examination.

STEELE. I can't.

PARSONS. I knew you'd say that!

STEELE. (*Baiting* PARSONS—*and enjoying it.*) Of course you knew it—if you knew anything. By the way—congratulations on the stage effects. (*Points to apparatus.*)

PARSONS. I don't want your irony—I want your help! It's terribly important. Why, her mother is Mrs. Robert Traherne of ——

STEELE. I don't give a damn who her mother is. (*Sits on table* R.) I'm leaving at one-thirty.

PARSONS. Put it off a day.

STEELE. Parsons, I've quit New York practice. I closed my office two weeks ago. And I've absolutely refused to see another patient. Sorry, but I can't make any exceptions.

PARSONS. But what's one day?

STEELE. Do you remember the day you were married?

PARSONS. Of course I do!

9

STEELE. Yes—but do you remember your—anticipation on that day?

PARSONS. Why—I—er—dammit —— Of course I do! (PARSONS *snorts.*)

STEELE. Well—(*Rises, crosses* L. C.) this is my day of days—and when I leave Grand Central I'm leaving a life that's over and done with, and I'm starting a new one —— I can't see her now—it's too late—but I have a few minutes and if it's of any help to talk over the case—fire ahead!

PARSONS. (*Apparently accepting defeat.*) Have you read the history?

STEELE. (*Picks up history.*) This gossip sheet?—" Widow of the late wire manufacturer."

PARSONS. Never mind about that now.

STEELE. All right, what's your diagnosis?

PARSONS. Frankly, I don't know. (*Sits* R. *of desk.*) But I do know the girl is desperately ill; I've been watching her like a hawk—and she's losing ground each day.

STEELE. Haven't you any line on it at all?

PARSONS. If I had to guess, I'd say some obscure internal injury—but I can't put my finger on it. There's nothing to go by—I can't get anything out of her.

STEELE. Won't talk—eh?

PARSONS. No—no co-operation.

STEELE. Is she usually irritable like this?

PARSONS. No—not ordinarily.

STEELE. You say she's been having persistent headaches? (*Sits* L. *of desk.*)

PARSONS. Yes. Ever since the accident.

STEELE. When did you first see her?

PARSONS. About an hour after she was thrown. She evidently rode home; had breakfast, and seemed all right. Then apparently she had a fainting spell.

STEELE. Did she actually faint or was she just very dizzy?

PARSONS. I couldn't make out. She resented my examination and wasn't very explicit.

STEELE. (*Looks at history.*) What's this about her heart?

PARSONS. My God, it was in awful shape—perfect ragtime ——

STEELE. Valvular?

PARSONS. No. Just very irregular—and she was perspiring quite a lot.

STEELE. Sounds like nicotine poisoning—probably smoked her head off the night before.

PARSONS. Nicoti —— Good Lord!

STEELE. What's the matter?

PARSONS. That's precisely what it was—nicotine poisoning—I never thought of it—but surely that ——

STEELE. You're quite right. (*Leans forward.*) That's not the *real* trouble.—You say she's a crack horsewoman?

PARSONS. The best.

STEELE. Then why was she thrown?

PARSONS. Well, it was a queer sort of accident. You see, she and a chap named Ronnie McVicker were riding cross-country —— They were making for an open gate. She was on his right. As they came near the gate, McVicker kept well over to the left to give her room; but instead of riding through the opening, she went head on for the fence—as though she hadn't seen it.

STEELE. (*For first time interested.*) What's that?

PARSONS. McVicker said she held her horse straight for the fence about six feet from the opening. Naturally the animal shied and threw her.

STEELE. You're *certain* she was on his *right* side?

PARSONS. Yes. Why?

STEELE. H'm —— (*Rises, paces down* L., *then back to desk chair.*) Why haven't you kept her in bed?

PARSONS. I've tried to.

STEELE. What do you mean?

PARSONS. You don't know that girl—why, yesterday she got up, went to lunch and the matinee and played contract all evening.

STEELE. What matinee?

PARSONS. Revival of " Cyrano," I think. Why?

STEELE. Oh, nothing. (*Sits on arm of chair.*)

PARSONS. No one can do anything with that girl. I'd have dropped the case weeks ago if it weren't that I'm an old family friend.

STEELE. How long have you known her?

PARSONS. I brought her into the world. I looked after her father when he died.

STEELE. I see. Well—on the whole I think your best bet's to get in touch with Findlay.

11

PARSONS. Findlay's in Europe.

STEELE. All right; then get Parke.

PARSONS. I don't want Parke or any of the rest of them. Dammit, they're no better than I am. I want you.

STEELE. Can't be done. (*Turns away.*)

PARSONS. Steele, I could cheerfully murder you!

STEELE. I'm sure you'd do it painlessly—in your best bedside manner and with real swagger—and who could ask more?

PARSONS. (*With great earnestness and force.*) Steele: you're always crying about the lack of human contact between doctor and patient.—Well, there's humanity waiting for you in that room— you can't turn your back on it now. (*Crosses to* STEELE C.)

STEELE. Why should I upset my plans for some spoiled, undisciplined Long Island flapper?

PARSONS. Because it's a doctor's business to cure sick people— because she'll die if you don't—because I'm an old friend of yours and I'm desperate. (*Pause.*)

STEELE. Very well—I'll see her—(PARSONS *registers relief*) but I warn you I'm going to catch that train. I'll do what I can. (*Walks L., calls through door.*) Miss Wainwright!

PARSONS. You're the court of last appeal.

STEELE. I can't promise anything. (*Enter* WAINWRIGHT, U. L.)

WAIN. Yes, Dr. Steele?

STEELE. Miss Wainwright, I'm going to see the patient.

WAIN. What?

STEELE. Our *last* case. Are my instruments ready?

WAIN. (*From now on she is strictly the professional nurse.*) Yes, sir.

STEELE. Can you manage that X-ray?

WAIN. Yes, Dr. Steele.

STEELE. I may want to use it. If so, I want just the wet plates. You can develop those in three minutes if you hurry.

WAIN. Yes, sir. (*Exits L.*)

PARSONS. You'll never know what this means to me, Steele.

STEELE. Let's see that history a minute. (*Picks up history.*)

PARSONS. Expecting the impossible: to make a diagnosis, I suppose?

STEELE. Can't say yet.

PARSONS. There's no hope if *you* can't.

STEELE. What did her father die of?

12

PARSONS. Bright's—arterial sclerosis; cardiac hypertrophy—but chiefly alcohol.

STEELE. No T. B. in the family?

PARSONS. None.

STEELE. I don't like the sound of this.

PARSONS. Steele, you must make her talk.

STEELE. I think we're ready now.

PARSONS. I'll get her—and, Steele, remember she's a bit spoiled—used to having her own way—you'll—you'll make allowances if she—well, you know —— (*Enter* WAINWRIGHT.)

STEELE. For God's sake, Parsons, bring the girl in and stop fussing. (*Exit* PARSONS R.) Everything set? (*To* WAINWRIGHT.)

WAIN. Yes, sir. (*Near door up* L.)

STEELE. When the patient comes in, I want you to take a lateral, and an A. P. I'll call you when I want the examining set.

WAIN. Yes, Dr. Steele.

STEELE. Wait! Pull those curtain things back, will you, please? I want a strong light on this chair. (*She pulls curtain on window* L. *He arranges chair* R. *of desk.*) Good! And when you take those pictures, get the plates developed faster than you ever did anything in your life. Then bring them in here—and no matter what happens, when it's time to go, you tell me.

WAIN. Yes, Dr. Steele. (*She exits* L. *Enter* JUDITH TRAHERNE. *A pause, a momentary suspension of action as she stands by door. Before any real awkwardness occurs, he goes to her.*)

STEELE. How do you do?

JUDITH. How do you do?

STEELE. (*Offers hand, she accepts it. He gives it a quick glance and continues to hold it.*) How did you get those?

JUDITH. What?

STEELE. Those burns. Right there—between the first two fingers.

JUDITH. That's funny—I never noticed them 'til now.

STEELE. H'mmm . . . (*Drops her hand.*)

JUDITH. (*Suddenly notices shadow box.*) What on earth is that?

STEELE. An X-ray shadow box.

JUDITH. So you've just taken my living-room and made it your office!

STEELE. That's right.—Won't you sit down?

JUDITH. (*Ironically.*) Thank you. (STEELE *goes to table, picks up*

13

history. JUDITH *looks at her hand, then at* STEELE, *shifts her position, waits. Finally.*) My name is Traherne.

STEELE. (*Not looking up.*) Mine's Steele.

JUDITH. Judith Traherne.

STEELE. Fred Steele.

JUDITH. (*Pause.*) Well, that's that. (*Everything* JUDITH *says carries a hidden challenge—as though she were daring* STEELE *to get anything out of her.*)

STEELE. Parsons tells me you're a great hunter.

JUDITH. Did you expect me to enter the living-room—excuse me, your office—leading a pack of hounds?

STEELE. I dunno. Look rather well. Scarlet coat against a background of books . . . (*She smiles a little—this doctor isn't so bad—at least he has a sense of humor.*) By the way, do you read them?

JUDITH. Not much, that is—not lately.

STEELE. Have your eyes been bothering you? (*He shifts the attack quickly. She's thinking, "I'll have to watch myself.*")

JUDITH. (*Pause, then definitely.*) No.

STEELE. I understand you don't like to talk about your health?

JUDITH. I do not.

STEELE. Any reason why?

JUDITH. It's a boring topic.

STEELE. I agree. Most people love it and I make my living by listening to them.

JUDITH. Then I'm afraid I'm wasting your time.

STEELE. Oh, don't worry. I'll send you a bill.

JUDITH. In that case I'll only be wasting my money, because there's nothing the matter with me; all this fuss over a little fall is beginning to get on my nerves!

STEELE. Does that light bother you? (*Makes as if to rise.*)

JUDITH. (*Rather more strongly than necessary.*) No.

STEELE. (*Settling back in his chair.*) How old are you, Miss Traherne?

JUDITH. Twenty-seven. I'm an only child. I weigh 125 pounds—stripped—I've had mumps, measles and whooping cough, all at the proper ages. I believe I have no congenital weakness—shall I go on?

STEELE. Please.

JUDITH. (*Lighting cigarette.*) My father drank himself to death;

14

my mother lives in Paris. If you're interested in knowing, we dislike one another cordially. My surroundings were and are thoroughly hygienic; a large airy duplex in New York, though we usually wintered at Aiken or Bermuda; summers on Long Island. I take a lot of exercise; I'm accustomed to a reasonable amount of tobacco and alcohol; I'm said to have a sense of humor. Now I think you have the medical background and the salient points of the family history. (*Again gesture of light bothering her.*)

STEELE. Do you use your eyes a great deal?

JUDITH. I generally keep them open, Doctor.

STEELE. Did you—by any chance—go to college, Miss Traherne?

JUDITH. Heavens, no—I'm totally uneducated—I mean it!

STEELE. What's the matter with education?

JUDITH. (*With concealed bitterness.*) There wasn't time for it, I guess.

STEELE. Why not?

JUDITH. Oh—the family were—a ——

STEELE. So it was their fault? I understand.

JUDITH. (*As though she had been trapped into saying something she would have preferred to keep to herself.*) No, it wasn't. They did very well by me. My own maids; my own horses; and cars; a couple of years at Foxcroft, a bit of Europe, and a very impressive debut at seventeen.

STEELE. (*Smiling—confidentially.*) What on earth do you do with yourself out here?

JUDITH. Oh, hunting—tennis—golf.

STEELE. Anything else?

JUDITH. Do you read the society column, Doctor?

STEELE. You mean " Mr. and Mrs. Numbskull entertained Mr. and Mrs. Flatfoot and friends at the Piping Rock Club "? That sort of stuff?

JUDITH. That sort of stuff, too. You know—shooting, yachting, parties, travel, gossip! All the pleasures of the idle rich. (*Pause. Then as she catches his look—defiantly.*) Well—I like it!

STEELE. Nonsense! It bores you to death and you know it. (*For a moment flame burns brightly.*)

JUDITH. Well—when that seems too tame, I raise the jumps and ride like hell!

STEELE. Yes,—that takes your mind off your mind—nicely. Doesn't it?

15

JUDITH. I haven't a particularly good mind.

STEELE. It appears reasonably sharp to me. (*Pause.*) How long do you think you can keep it up?

JUDITH. Keep what up? (*She knows what he means.*)

STEELE. Repeating the same old stale rounds and pretending you're satisfied with them.

JUDITH. Everyone pretends. The whole game is one of pretense, so why be sentimental about it? I'm not complaining; as I think of it I've been dealt a very good hand. I'm young, I've no particular responsibilities and I shan't cultivate them either; one is freer without. If certain things work out, I shall probably marry a very attractive man I know. When I do we'll build a big house on a ridge with a glorious view. He'll have his polo and I'll have my hunting; with luck we'll have about forty years of it. I think that's a pretty good setup.

STEELE. Do you?

JUDITH. Yes, I do. It seems to me a very pleasant and well-conceived plan of life—and wisely stripped of too many illusions.—You don't think much of that, do you?

STEELE. Not much.

JUDITH. Why? Just why?

STEELE. I think what you call illusions are the only important things in the world. Not many people have them, and I think that anyone who has, and who deliberatley smashes them—isn't worth one little damn.

JUDITH. (*Bridling.*) What right have you to criticize me?

STEELE. None whatever. You asked for my opinion and I gave it. It's probably of no importance, so don't let it worry you.

JUDITH. Well, then, what right have you to be so cocksure of *yourself?*

STEELE. No right, if I were to force my views on others. Every right where they concern me alone.

JUDITH. Don't you care anything for the world's opinion?

STEELE. I think it less important than one's own.

JUDITH. You're the most conceited man I ever met.

STEELE. You go your way—let me go mine. Our paths aren't likely to cross again. The world's big enough for both of us.

JUDITH. Anyway, that's my racket. What's yours? (*Pause—then sharply.*) Come, now, you've cross-questioned me—it's only fair to take your own medicine.

STEELE. High pressure surgery; Park Avenue clientele—about ten days off each summer.

JUDITH. It sounds perfectly awful.

STEELE. It is.

JUDITH. Why do you do it?

STEELE. Because, like you, I've been caught in a racket.

JUDITH. What a relief! Why, you're no better than I am.

STEELE. But I'm quitting—clearing out.

JUDITH. Where are you going?

STEELE. A little town in northern Vermont.

JUDITH. Vermont?—You mean that narrow little pinched-up State on the wrong side of Boston? What on earth are you going to do up *there?*

STEELE. I'm going to live there and be a country doctor.

JUDITH. In heaven's name—WHY!

STEELE. Because I've messed things up rather badly in New York.

JUDITH. I thought you were at the top of your profession.

STEELE. I have no profession—here. I'm nothing but an efficient, impersonal machine, and so busy doing my petty job that I've never had time to be a physician. I couldn't recognize most of my patients six months later—except by their scars.

JUDITH. Why should you want to?

STEELE. Do you seriously imagine that a doctor's job ends on the operating table? Have you any idea of what being a physician means?

JUDITH. I've never thought much about it.

STEELE. (*After short pause.*) I suppose it's the most comprehensive job on earth, because it means caring for the complete human being—not just his body. It means sympathy with human suffering, understanding of human despair, knowledge of human weakness, and the power of helping.

JUDITH. But the old family physician is a thing of the past. He's as dead as the Dodo.

STEELE. Yes—and so is the physician's craft—gone. Nothing left of it. Where do you find men today like Osler, with his humanity and wisdom and love for his patients?

JUDITH. Ah, a moralist as well as a surgeon! I'm beginning to suspect, Dr. Steele, that we belong to different generations. I remember my grandmother talking in very much the same way. Such a delightful Victorian, my grandmother. All lace and ruffles and propriety. You and she would have had a charming time together over the tea table. She also believed the world was a good place and that life had a clear and noble purpose.—Forgive me, Doctor, if I'm putting words into your mouth, but that's what you do believe, isn't it? .

STEELE. I believe that a universe is a damned exciting place to be alive in.

JUDITH. Why, may I ask?

STEELE. I thought you kept your eyes open.

JUDITH. Meaning——?

STEELE. Meaning that unless you're congenitally blind or completely drugged, the answer is all around you staring you in the face.

JUDITH. You mean the universe?

STEELE. Yes—full of hidden mystery and beauty and incredible vitality, and so exquisitely balanced and ordered.

JUDITH. Frankly it seems to me rather haphazard.

STEELE. Haphazard my eye! Take a look through a microscope some time at a drop of stagnant water if you think that. Study the human nervous system for a while. Find out what the geologist knows, and what the astronomer doesn't know.

JUDITH. And just what will I discover from this course of study, Dr. Steele?

STEELE. You'll discover that from a grain of wheat germinating in the earth to the farthest island universe, there's order—rigid and absolute; order that's majestic, convincing, overwhelming.

JUDITH. Well, I'm overwhelmed, Doctor, though still unconvinced, but will you please tell me, if it's all so beautifully ordered, where do the hidden mystery and beauty come in?

STEELE. Perhaps you can tell me what it was that made Shakespeare write his plays? Or El Greco paint those strange canvases; or how the architect of the Parthenon developed his magic sense for balance. Then go a little deeper and tell me why Socrates quietly drank poison rather than give up teaching the young men of Athens; find out what Christ thought about in the desert—and then come back here and get off some more cheap wise-cracks at the Victorians and the noble purpose of life—if you still feel like it.

JUDITH. I realize I'm being thoroughly spanked, Dr. Steele, but wouldn't it save time and energy if you'd just explain the significance of the mysterious universe to me?

STEELE. I don't know what it signifies. I don't even know if it's good or evil. But I do recognize its stature, and I think it's important to find one's niche in the scheme of things.

JUDITH. And just how does one go about that?

STEELE. It doesn't make a scrap of difference so long as what you're doing seems important to you—so long as you're moving in some direction that your own imagination and your own intelligence compel you to move in.

JUDITH. That's putting a tremendous premium on your own intelligence.

STEELE. No, it's putting the premium on vitality, for it means having a sense of excitement and curiosity, it means being alive, it means functioning, burning up energy—the actual job can be as simple as you like so long as you're on fire to do it . . . for instance, I think a fine salmon working upstream against the current —fighting every foot of the river merely to find a spawning bed and then to get back to the sea—is doing its job a darned sight better than most of us.

JUDITH. Even if it gets caught on the way?

STEELE. I'm not talking about safety; I'm not even talking about success as it's usually thought of.

JUDITH. Don't you consider that of any importance?

STEELE. What does it amount to? Acquiring certain things that other people think you ought to want—money, prestige ——

JUDITH. And power.

STEELE. Exactly. And how many people do you know who have the character to stand that kind of success?

JUDITH. Oh, I admit most of them are pretty pompous.

STEELE. Do you know why?—Because they're diseased. They're shot through with the most deadly virus on earth: intrenched complacency. And that means atrophy, and atrophy means just one thing—death.

JUDITH. I've never thought of success that way before . . . but you haven't answered my question . . . where is my place in the scheme of things?

STEELE. (Quietly.) You know I can't answer that.

JUDITH. Why not?—You seem to know all the answers.

STEELE. Only the problems—unfortunately. And there are plenty of them. I'm hoping to find the answer to some of them up in Vermont.

19

JUDITH. (*For first time with absolute sincerity and simplicity.*) Why are you a doctor?

STEELE. You're too young to remember the war.

JUDITH. What happened?

STEELE. There's no point in going into that.

JUDITH. Please tell me—please.

STEELE. I was a farmer's son in this same town I'm going back to —a typical Vermont farm—with just a bare living in it. By scraping together every penny they could my people sent me to college. I was nineteen at the time of the war and a Junior at Dartmouth. It's hard to explain to anyone who wasn't there what those war years were like. I suppose we were all a little crazy. Many people honestly believed the propaganda; that it was a war to end all wars. I believed it, so I signed up and was sent over in the infantry. Then came the reality; the rotten business of killing—the beastliness of it all and the futility. During the Meuse-Argonne show I picked up a nasty piece of shrapnel in my right knee. The doctor at the base wasn't fit to be a veterinary. He infected the wound doing a simple dressing. Then I was in for it. I don't know how long I was there, but it went on for weeks and weeks and every morning that doctor with his dreadful probe. Finally he told me they were going to have to amputate my leg. He wasn't very tactful about it. I told him not to bother, that I wanted to die. I don't remember his answer, for at that moment I noticed someone else was standing there—someone whom I'd not seen before. He wore a colonel's uniform. I was told later that he was the chief surgeon of the Division, who was making rounds. He asked the doctor if he could look at me. I'll never forget his face; there was great strength and great gentleness in it. The minute he spoke I knew he was a New Englander—he had that flat A we all have. He asked me where I came from and said he knew the country like a book, that he'd fished the Felsboro River ever since he was a kid. We talked about the different flies we used on the Willow Dale pool; of the incredible green of the water and the peace of the hills. Then he said, " This war isn't going to last forever, but the mountains are still there and the trout will be running; you're going back there to catch them." Then he examined me. I've never known such hands or such dexterity. He told me he thought he could save my leg. " But I'll have to do it now," he said. " I must be in Paris tonight. I'll scrub up at once." Just as he left, he

20

turned and said: "Good luck." I never saw him again, but I learned then what the power of a physician could be.—It's why I'm a doctor.

JUDITH. Thank you for telling me that. I understand now why you're going away.—It must be wonderful to be doing what you really believe in.

STEELE. Don't you?

JUDITH. I don't know what I believe in.

STEELE. Youth—beauty—money.—The world is at your feet, isn't it?

JUDITH. And I intend to explore it!

STEELE. All?

JUDITH. Why not? I'm young. And I want to see it all—the whole show. Everything!

STEELE. I know of some bad spots.

JUDITH. I'll risk that. I like taking chances. That's part of the fun, and I'm going to get all the excitement that's going. I'd like to get into one of those bad spots, and then out again under my own steam. I want to try everything; I want every sensation and every experience there is.

STEELE. What else do you want?

JUDITH. Have I left anything out?

STEELE. Haven't you?

JUDITH. (*Throwing discretion to the winds.*) Yes! I don't mind telling you: I want admiration! I want gaiety and music and dancing. I want people to look at me. I want to be the center of attraction. I want—I—I guess I want the earth!—Oh, damn!

STEELE. What's the matter?

JUDITH. I haven't done this in years. . . . I don't know why I did it!

STEELE. Did what?

JUDITH. Talked—slopped over!

STEELE. We all need to do that occasionally.

JUDITH. This is your fault! You led me on by talking the way you did. Do you do this with all your patients?

STEELE. I'd forgotten you *were* my patient.

JUDITH. (*Pettishly.*) Well, I'm not here for a social visit! (*Again that gesture as though the light bothered her.*)

STEELE. (*Rising.*) That light is in your eyes.

21

JUDITH. Why do you keep insisting on that? There's nothing the matter with my eyes.

STEELE. You're squinting.

JUDITH. I'm not squinting!

STEELE. (*Pulling curtains together.*) There, that's better.

JUDITH. Suit yourself; it's *your office!*

STEELE. (*He sits on arm of chair* L. *of desk.*) What did you do yesterday?

JUDITH. I played bridge in the afternoon. I went to the theater in the evening.

STEELE. Other way around, wasn't it?

JUDITH. Why—yes. I guess it was.

STEELE. What was the play?

JUDITH. Er——

STEELE. "Cyrano," wasn't it?

JUDITH. Yes, why?

STEELE. Did you like it?

JUDITH. My head was aching so, I thought Cyrano would never die.

STEELE. How long have you had these headaches?

JUDITH. Oh, I—I don't have them.

STEELE. You have one now.

JUDITH. No! I have not!

STEELE. Very well. How did you come out at bridge yesterday?

JUDITH. Let me think——

STEELE. Quickly!

JUDITH. I can't remember.

STEELE. You lost.

JUDITH. Yes, I did lose.

STEELE. How much?

JUDITH. How can I remember! I play bridge every day.

STEELE. You've been losing a lot lately, haven't you?

JUDITH. Yes.

STEELE. Playing badly?

JUDITH. I suppose so.

STEELE. Forgetting what cards are out; and what's been bid.

JUDITH. (*Angrily.*) Why do you ask me these silly questions?

STEELE. Wait! Did Parsons say you might go out yesterday?

JUDITH. I'm accustomed to look after myself, Doctor.

STEELE. But you did disobey his orders, didn't you?

JUDITH. What if I did?

STEELE. Why pay a doctor to advise you and then disregard his advice?

JUDITH. I didn't want a doctor! Someone else called him!

STEELE. So you are taking orders from someone else, are you?

JUDITH. Listen, Doctor. Ever since I've been financially independent I've never " taken orders " from anyone, and as long as I live, I'll never take orders—from anyone. And here's something else. I'm well, absolutely well! I'm young and strong and nothing can touch me—neither you nor Dr. Parsons can make an invalid out of me! And now, I'll ask you to excuse me. (*Rises.*) I'm sorry to have wasted so much of your time but this is my last interview with doctors! (STEELE *has risen*—JUDITH *starts to go up* R.)

STEELE. Yes! You're running away: you're frightened. That's why you held certain things back from Dr. Parsons. You were afraid to admit them.

JUDITH. That isn't true! (*Crosses* L. *again.*)

STEELE. Oh, yes it is! You didn't tell him that you'd been having these headaches for months—but you have. And they've been getting worse lately, until now you're never free of them. And your eyes have been acting queerly, too. Just as though someone was shutting a pair of folding doors. (*He brings edges of his hands together to illustrate.*) Until your vision is almost cut in half. You pretended it was imagination, but it wasn't. Then that queer, dull feeling in your right arm. You couldn't laugh that off. I'll tell you how you got those burns—a cigarette! It burned your fingers, and you never felt it, because your tactile nerves are paralyzed. Your memory is all shot to pieces. You can't concentrate. Look at your bridge scores! You're irritable because your nerves are on edge. You're afraid to admit it, but you can't deny it.

JUDITH. It's a lie! I'm well! Why do you bully me like this?

STEELE. Because I want to help you. I can't possibly do it unless I can get you to talk. (JUDITH *sits down again.*) Good! I knew I could count on you. (*Calls.*) Miss Wainwright! Just give me your right hand please.—Now the left.—Now squeeze—tight—good and tight.—Thank you. (WAINWRIGHT *enters with tray of instruments. Puts them on upper end of desk.*) Would you mind taking off your coat? Just give me your right elbow, please, in my hand. Just relax—good. (*He tests with reflex hammer, which he*

23

takes from tray on desk.) Now the other one. Good. (Repeats test.) Cross your knees, please. (Tests with hammer.)

JUDITH. (Laughing at knee reflex.) That always makes me laugh.

STEELE. Silly, isn't it? Now the other one. (Repeats knee test.) Now the Achilles. (Holds her foot, taps back of her ankle.) Good. Now the other one. (Repeats test.) Good. Good. (Takes pencil flashlight from WAINWRIGHT.) Don't worry, it's just an electric torch. (Examines pupils of her eyes with flashlight. Keeps hand well cupped to shade each eye.) Would you mind looking up toward the ceiling?—H'm —— (Examines R. eye first, then L. eye.) Just look up, please. (Examines her eyes and nose with flashlight. Puts finger against tip of her nose.) Look at the tip of your nose. Right at my finger. Up—down—up—down.—Good. (Gives flashlight to WAINWRIGHT—takes ophthalmoscope. Tests ophthalmoscope light and focus on palm of his hand. Uses L. hand on instrument for L. eye—R. hand for R. eye. Examines R. eye first.) Now we'll get a little closer view.—Just look over here, will you, please?—A little to the left and up. Good. (Examines pupil—sees there is a defect—looks at WAINWRIGHT.) Just once again. (Examines pupil again. Then crosses below JUDITH to examine L. eye.) Just steady. No—look up there and to the right. Thank you. (WAINWRIGHT takes ophthalmoscope, puts it back on tray. Hands him a small cube.) Would you mind closing your eyes for a minute? Hold out both hands with the palms upward. (Puts cube into her L. hand.) Can you tell me what that is?

JUDITH. It's a cube.

STEELE. Is it hard or soft?

JUDITH. Hard. (He transfers cube to her R. hand.)

STEELE. Now what's this?

JUDITH. I'm not quite sure.

STEELE. (Takes cube and substitutes pencil in her R. hand.) What's this? Turn it over in your fingers—what shape is it?

JUDITH. I can't quite make out.

STEELE. (Places pencil in her L. hand.) Now? Can you tell me what this is?

JUDITH. A pencil.

STEELE. Right!

JUDITH. May I open my eyes now?

STEELE. No, just a minute. (He puts piece of silk in her L. hand.) Is that cloth rough or smooth?

24

JUDITH. It's a piece of silk.

STEELE. I'm going to fool you this time—now, what's this? (*He substitutes piece of burlap—places it in her R. hand.*)

JUDITH. Still silk.

STEELE. (*Puts burlap back on tray.*) You can open your eyes now. (*He pulls small chair over L. in front of her. Sits down.*) Just uncross your knees, please. Sit up straight. Now, I'm going to hold out my hands like this, (*Stretches out both arms.*) and ask you to close one eye, then I will move my hands in and I want you to stop me quickly when they come within your range of vision. Would you mind closing your left eye? That's it, just cup it—don't press—and stop me very quickly with this hand (*Indicates her R. hand.*) when you see my hands moving in. Ready? (*Again stretches out his arms and slowly moves hands in until they come within range of vision. She cannot see to R. in either eye—therefore fails to see approach of his L. hand.*) Good. Now again—this time with the left hand. Now let's do the same with the other eye. Ready. (*Repeats same business.*) Good. That's all. (*Rises, puts chair C. again, crosses L. of desk.*) Just two more questions. How long ago did you first notice these headaches?

JUDITH. Oh, months ago. Five or six.

STEELE. Have your eyes bothered you as long as that?

JUDITH. No. That's only lately. The last few weeks.

STEELE. Splendid. That's a great help. I'm going to ask you to go into that room where the nurse will take some X-rays.

WAIN. Will you come with me, Miss Traherne, please?

JUDITH. Certainly. (JUDITH *exits.*)

WAIN. (*At door L. C.*) It's time to go.

STEELE. Make those pictures good and sharp.

WAIN. Yes, Dr. Steele. (*Exit* WAINWRIGHT L. C. STEELE *raises shade* L. *Crosses* R.—*opens door and calls* PARSONS.)

STEELE. Dr. Parsons! (PARSONS *enters.* STEELE *crosses to* R. C., *followed by* PARSONS.)

PARSONS. Well?

STEELE. Got it.

PARSONS. Thank God.

STEELE. I shouldn't.

PARSONS. What do you mean? What is it?

STEELE. Brain tumor. Glioma of the brain.

PARSONS. Good God! Where?

25

STEELE. In the temporal and parietal lobes. She has a right visual defect.

PARSONS. You're having her X-rayed?

STEELE. The plates won't show much, but I think they'll confirm what I say.

PARSONS. Is it operable?

STEELE. With luck, yes.

PARSONS. Good enough.

STEELE. But—if the plates show that it's diffused, as I think it is ——

PARSONS. She'll get a recurrence.

STEELE. Yes.

PARSONS. And that means ——?

STEELE. About ten months to a year.

PARSONS. Invalidism, I suppose?

STEELE. No, that's the one decent thing about it. She'll probably never know until the last. Then she'll go blind.

PARSONS. Amblyopia?

STEELE. Yes—of course her blindness (*A pace toward* PARSONS) will only last for a minute, but that's the signal.—There'll be only a few hours after that ——

PARSONS. Are you going to tell her?

STEELE. Would you want her to know?

PARSONS. No.

STEELE. That's the answer.

PARSONS. Poor child. (WAINWRIGHT *enters with wet plates—crosses to* STEELE.)

STEELE. Yeah. (*Switches on shadow box.*) Give me the lateral. (STEELE *holds plate before ground glass.*) That doesn't show much, but it looks suspicious.—Now the A. P. (*Holds second plate before glass—studies it carefully.*) Look here! See that?

PARSONS. That shadow?

STEELE. Yes—notice the difference in density.

PARSONS. That means calcification, doesn't it?

STEELE. Yes. (WAINWRIGHT *exits* L. *with plates.* STEELE *switches off shadow box.*)

PARSONS. Dammit, Steele! Don't stand there looking like that!

STEELE. Rotten business, doctoring.

PARSONS. I know. But, after all, we've both seen young people die.

STEELE. Yes. But a girl like this—who's so terribly alive and who's so entitled to live—God! to have this thing—this contemptible, meaningless organism, come along, and put a period to it.—(*Angry.*) Why did you have to call me in on this case?

WAIN. (*Enters, interrupting.*) The patient is ready, Dr. Steele. But we'll have to leave at once if you're going to catch your train.

STEELE. Train? Forget it! (JUDITH *enters.* STEELE *points to a chair.*) Sit down. (*She sits.*) You must be done up after all this questioning and examining. (PARSONS *sits on sofa.*)

JUDITH. Just a bit. Sorry I was so childish.

STEELE. I liked the way you fought back at me. You're a good sport.

JUDITH. If I weren't, Doctor, I'm afraid I wouldn't be much of anything.

STEELE. I shan't accept that statement. But it's going to help immensely. (*Sits* C.) I'm afraid this may be something of a shock to you, but it's only the idea that's hard to accept, not the thing itself. You see, something's gone wrong in that incredible labyrinth of wires, the brain.

JUDITH. The brain!

STEELE. The brain is like any other part of the body; things get out of kilter, and have to be adjusted.

JUDITH. Exactly what is this thing?

STEELE. The technical name is Glioma.

JUDITH. Sounds like a kind of plant.

STEELE. It *is* rather like a plant—a parasitic one.

JUDITH. Doctor—what does " adjusted " mean?

STEELE. I'm afraid it means an operation.

JUDITH. Oh, that's absurd.

STEELE. You've got to face it.

JUDITH. I don't believe it! Are you *positive?* I won't have an operation! (*Crosses to* PARSONS, *who puts arm around her.*) I won't let you. Do you hear? (*Pause.*) It must be pretty serious.

STEELE. It is—very, very serious. It's going to take our combined efforts to beat this thing. I shall need all the help you can give me, Miss Traherne.

JUDITH. That I can give you?

STEELE. Yes—confidence and hope are more than surgery. You must trust me, completely, absolutely. You'll need all your energy. We can't afford to waste the hundredth part of an ounce of that, I must have your complete faith.

27

JUDITH. I'm afraid faith isn't my long suit.

STEELE. From now on it's going to be, and in return I'll give you all the skill and intelligence at my command—remember, you're putting yourself entirely in my hands. I'm doing all the worrying, all the thinking. Your job is to *trust* me.

JUDITH. (*Moves toward* STEELE.) I do trust you.

STEELE. I hoped you would. When can you be ready?

JUDITH. I'm in your hands, Doctor.

STEELE. I must check certain things. We won't operate until the day after tomorrow, but I'm going to take you to the hospital this afternoon. I want you to get all the rest you can. I'll call for you, let's say—three o'clock.

JUDITH. All right, three o'clock. Doctor, it won't leave a scar?

STEELE. I'll see that it doesn't.

JUDITH. You're giving up all your plans for me.

STEELE. I'm doing what I want to do.

JUDITH. I wish we'd met before, Doctor.

STEELE. So do I.

JUDITH. And yet you'd be an awful frost at a party.

STEELE. Terrible. I don't belong at parties.

JUDITH. No, you don't. How long will I have to be in the hospital?

STEELE. Oh, about six weeks.

JUDITH. I suppose you'll let me ride as soon as I get out?

STEELE. I think we'll put that off a little longer.

JUDITH. *How* long?

STEELE. I couldn't say exactly. Suppose we talk that over later?

JUDITH. Why not now?

STEELE. Our first job is to bring you through the operation and start you on the road to recovery.

JUDITH. It's beginning to sound like a long road. Doctor, you said it was *very* serious?

STEELE. Yes.

JUDITH. You also said I'd be convalescent in six weeks.

STEELE. About that.

JUDITH. After that, will I be able to live a completely normal life?

STEELE. Yes. Of course it'll take some time for you to get your strength back.

JUDITH. Will this operation absolutely cure me?

STEELE. I think I can guarantee that you will make a complete surgical recovery.

JUDITH. " A complete surgical recovery? " What does that mean?

STEELE. It means that you will get well. No worries now?

JUDITH. None—I just wanted to be sure I knew the truth. That you weren't keeping anything back from me. I do now—you see, I trust you. (*They shake hands.*)

STEELE. Good luck. (STEELE *starts to exit* R. PARSONS *follows him.*)

PARSONS. I'll be right back, Judith.

CURTAIN

ACT II

Scene 1

The same. Three months later. At rise of curtain we find ALDEN BLAINE, BILL EWING, *and his wife,* CONNIE.

ALDEN. My dear, publishers are like that. They descend on you without warning, and they insist upon being entertained.

CONNIE. But, Alden, we've asked Joe and Florence over for bridge.

ALDEN. Call them up and tell them you can't have them.

BILL. I know, sweetheart, but we invited 'em a week ago. Besides, they don't—well, they don't go out very often.

ALDEN. Why should they? They haven't a damn thing to offer except money—which I suspect he made crookedly.

CONNIE. But I can't hurt her feelings—can I?

ALDEN. Precisely, Connie. She wouldn't know it if you hit her with a club. I know, my dear: I've done it.

CONNIE. I thought you used poisoned arrows—exclusively.

ALDEN. Darts, my pet, smaller and more effective.

BILL. Has this publisher of yours actually arrived?

ALDEN. Arrived: and asleep in the living-room.

CONNIE. It never occurred to me that publishers slept.

ALDEN. That's when they pick most of their books. . . . Now, I'm counting on you for tonight. If I can only get Judith, I'm saved.

BILL. Judith would save any party.

ALDEN. I know, Bill dear—Judith is built that way!

CONNIE. Her operation did wonders for her. She's absolutely radiant—more so than ever.

ALDEN. Do you know why? . . . She's . . . No! . . . I won't gossip about Judith. . . .

CONNIE. Alden, you disappoint me.

ALDEN. Quite right, I have a rotten tongue and I like using it. But Judith Traherne is the one person in this world I really love.

BILL. Check.

CONNIE. Double-check. (*Enter* JANETTE BORDEN. *Pretty, twenty-five, dressed in tennis shorts, carries a racquette.*)

JANETTE. Check again—hello, everybody, and where's Judith?

ALDEN. Feeding Pegasus ambrosia—in other words, out riding; nobody knows when she'll be back and what the hell are you doing here?

JANETTE. Hoping for a cocktail.

BILL. Ride along with us; we're going in a minute.

CONNIE. Where's Pete?

JANETTE. Pete and I aren't speaking today. In fact Pete's in no condition to speak. I've been working over him with ice-packs since six A. M.

ALDEN. Have you tried Benzedrene?

JANETTE. No joking, Alden, he has the god-awfullest hangover I've ever seen, and I speak as an expert.

ALDEN. Check and double-check.

JANETTE. (*Thumbs her nose at* ALDEN.) When he came to this morning and saw the green stripes on his black pajamas . . . (*Imitates snake's motion.*) well, Pete thought he had 'em again, and so did I.

BILL. He was making heavy weather of it the last I saw of him.

CONNIE. He kept insisting he was an admiral.

JANETTE. The louse!

BILL. And at about three-minute intervals he'd heave what he called a "depth-bomb" into himself.—When I left he was listing at an angle of forty-five degrees.

JANETTE. Well, he sank—shortly thereafter. And when he came up from the bottom this morning—he was no admiral. . . . I left him tapering off on warm milk and I'm going back shortly to hear his prayers.

CONNIE. Poor Janette, it's been an exhausting day. I should think you needed a cocktail.—Come on, Bill, straight home—and straight Martinis. I don't want any amateur experiments with high explosives.

JANETTE. Don't worry, Connie, I'll watch him like a hawk. (*They start for door.*)

ALDEN. I'm afraid the simile is too accurate to be reassuring—to Connie.

JANETTE. (*Pleasantly.*) Alden—you're a bitch.

ALDEN. I'm a novelist.—Eight o'clock, Connie.

CONNIE. Right. Tell Judith we called. (*They go out.* ALDEN *rings bell. Picks up a book, smiles.*) One of my own rotten novels!

31

(*Enter* MAID.) Josie—a large brandy and soda, please.

JOSIE. I was just bringing the tray in, Mrs. Blaine, when they left.

ALDEN. Good.

JOSIE. Mrs. Blaine, I have a telegram for Miss Traherne. It came two hours ago.

ALDEN. Leave it on the table.

JOSIE. Yes, Mrs. Blaine. (*Exit* JOSIE.)

ALDEN. (*Goes to table, picks up telegram, holds it up carefully to light, scrutinizes it.*) Damn—why do they always fold them that way! (*Puts it down. Goes to window.* JOSIE *re-enters with brandy in tall glass and bottle of soda.*) Thanks, Josie. Is Miss Traherne dining out?

JOSIE. No, ma'am.

ALDEN. Anyone coming here?

JOSIE. She ordered dinner for two, but she didn't know if the party would be coming for sure ——

ALDEN. The "party" being—who, Josie?

JOSIE. Miss Traherne didn't say, but I—well, I ——

ALDEN. Ye-es?

JOSIE. I *think* it might be the Doctor.

ALDEN. I'm sure it will be the Doctor —— Damn! . . . I'll leave a note for her ——

JOSIE. Yes, Mrs. Blaine. (*Starts for door.*)

ALDEN. I'm sorry not to see her.

JOSIE. You should be.—She looked lovely in her habit. Did you know it was her first ride? You should have seen her on that horse, Mrs. Blaine.

ALDEN. (*Writing.*) Don't, Josie.—I hate horses.

JOSIE. Very good, Mrs. Blaine. (*Exit.*)

ALDEN. Besides, I never look at one that it doesn't immediately do something that embarrasses me. (*Off-stage sound. A moment later enter* JUDITH *in her riding habit. She looks radiant and young.*) Darling!

JUDITH. Alden!

ALDEN. I was scribbling you a note; I have messages of love from Connie, Bill and Janette. They've just left.

JUDITH. I saw their car on my way up from the stables.—Have you been here long?

ALDEN. Hours.

JUDITH. Terribly sorry.

32

ALDEN. You look it! (JUDITH *lights cigarette.*)

JUDITH. Oh, Alden, it's been a gorgeous day—fruit blossoms all out—horse-chestnuts—tulips—the time went so quick.—That reminds me! (*Rises, goes to bell, rings.*) There's something I have to say to that new head groom.—Didn't Josie offer you anything to drink?

ALDEN. (*Points to brandy.*) I asked for it.

JUDITH. My dear, the worst thing about going to a hospital is that the anesthetic seems to paralyze your household. (*Sits.*)

ALDEN. How was the ride?

JUDITH. I was nervous at first. I couldn't forget the day I crashed the fence, but then I put my mare to a hedge—we cleared it beautifully, and the fields ahead were clear and green—and I was free.—What amuses you so?

ALDEN. I'm very pleased with you.

JUDITH. Me? Why?

ALDEN. You're such a decided improvement over your old self.

JUDITH. Am I?

ALDEN. They did more than give you a new brain—they gave you a new disposition as well.

JUDITH. Now what the hell was the matter with my disposition?

ALDEN. I've always loved you, but always despite your faults. (*Enter* JOSIE.)

JUDITH. Oh, Josie, tell Michael to come here right away.

JOSIE. I'll try to find him at once, Miss Traherne.

JUDITH. I'm sure you'll find him.—(*Exit* JOSIE.) You should see him—six feet, *and* with an air.—But what were you writing me? Not important, was it?

ALDEN. Very. I've been deliberately putting you in a good humor. I want you for dinner at eight tonight—to seduce my publisher. He's being nasty about my new book—says the public's no longer interested in sex; the truth is he's forty-eight and a little jaded and he needs to meet someone who is alluring and dangerous—which is you. There'll be quantities of the best champagne and I'm not going to be refused!

JUDITH. Alden, I can't.

ALDEN. So he's coming for dinner?

JUDITH. Who?

ALDEN. Your Doctor.

JUDITH. My ——? How did you know?

33

ALDEN. I'm a novelist, besides I've been snooping. You'll have to put him off for a day.

JUDITH. He's leaving for Vermont tomorrow, but he may not get here till after dinner; he said he'd —— (MICHAEL, *head groom, appears at doorway and knocks. He is, as* JUDITH *suggested, tall and handsome.*)

MICHAEL. You wanted to see me, Miss Traherne?

JUDITH. I don't like the way Red Queen behaved.

MICHAEL. She hasn't been ridden enough.

JUDITH. She's been handled roughly. She's not used to that.

MICHAEL. If you don't mind my saying so, Miss Traherne, that horse has been a bit spoiled.

JUDITH. I do mind your saying so! (*Pause: no yielding on either side.*) Michael, have you ridden her on a curb bit?

MICHAEL. I have that.

JUDITH. Well, don't you ever do it again as long as you live!

MICHAEL. Why, that mare's no more than a filly—and she's a natural cut-up. I put a curb on her just to let her know it was there.

JUDITH. You ought to know better. Her mouth's too sensitive.

MICHAEL. Don't I know? It's like velvet—ye can go over it with a glass and ye'll not see a mark on it. I handled her as light on that curb as you would on a snaffle; but she needed a lesson and I gave it to her.

JUDITH. You'll not do that again!

MICHAEL. Sorry, Miss Traherne, but ye'd better leave the handling of the horses to me. I'm in charge of the stables. A month from now and ye don't like the way things is goin'—you can fire me.

JUDITH. Believe me—I will!

MICHAEL. Ye'll not be firin' me, Miss Judith. We're goin' to get on together. (*Exit* MICHAEL.)

JUDITH. Hasn't much confidence, has he? The worst of it is I know he's right.

ALDEN. If I were a horse—I'd recognize that in his eye which I would call " master."—God! If only I had *him* for a publisher! Incidentally, you'd better watch out.

JUDITH. I'm always at my best on my own five-yard line.

ALDEN. I guess you're safe at the moment with —— Oh, by the way, there's a telegram for you.

JUDITH. Where?

ALDEN. (*Handing it to her.*) Here.

JUDITH. Why didn't you tell me!

ALDEN. I know it's bad news for me.

JUDITH. (*Tears it open—excitedly.*) Alden!—He's coming! Any minute!—You beast, Alden, for not giving it to me at once!

ALDEN. You've been pretty hard hit, haven't you?

JUDITH. (*With deep sincerity.*) Alden —— (*Pause.*) Alden, I ——

ALDEN. (*Affectionately.*) Go on, say it.

JUDITH. (*Hand on* ALDEN'S *hand.*) What can I say? It can't be talked about: nothing like this ever happened to me before. I don't think it ever happened to anyone else either. Am I silly? Am I crazy?

ALDEN. (*Sincerely.*) I think, my darling, that this time it's the real thing.

JUDITH. (*Impulsively, genuinely.*) Oh, it is, Alden. I know it: I *am*—I am in love with him.

ALDEN. And he? That's always the first question.

JUDITH. I don't know.

ALDEN. You should know. You've had enough men in love with you.

JUDITH. *They* haven't helped me understand *him*. He's a strange person, Alden, a marvelous person when you get to know him, but he's so hard to see into. He keeps his real self hidden so deeply away.—Oh, he's *conscious* of me, I'm sure of that. (*Rises.*) I affect him pleasantly. (*Crosses to sofa—sits.*)

ALDEN. That *sounds* a trifle like understatement to me.

JUDITH. It *may* be much more. I don't know. I'm so afraid of reading into his speech and manner what I'd like to see there that I lean over backwards. . . . He *may* be in love with me, Alden— I don't know whether he even admits his emotions to himself.

ALDEN. Why couldn't the Spaniards or the French have landed on Plymouth Rock instead of the Puritans?

JUDITH. He does like being with me; that I know: he's a softer, warmer person. We've talked endlessly—he's given me hours of his time—he could have left a few days after the operation but he stayed on. He's opened my eyes to a new world—he's the first thoroughly fine person I've ever come close to.—Why aren't you laughing? I can't help laughing at myself for feeling this way.

ALDEN. (*Rises, crosses to end table by sofa.*) I'm not so sure I oughtn't to cry.

35

JUDITH. Oh, Alden. I want him. Maybe—I hope—I'd be good for him, too—but it will take time. (*She sees that* ALDEN *looks grave.*) You don't think so?

ALDEN. I think I hope you don't.

JUDITH. (*Sharply.*) Why?

ALDEN. English is your common tongue; but what else have you in common?

JUDITH. Compatibility goes much deeper than playing the same system at bridge, and liking the same kind of cocktails.

ALDEN. Sometimes I'm not sure—besides —— What about Vermont?

JUDITH. I'm afraid Vermont and I won't understand each other very well.

ALDEN. (*Winks.*) " Point number one—said the bi-colored Rock-snake Python."

JUDITH. He'll come back—some day—if I'm sufficiently wise.

ALDEN. Think so?

JUDITH. I admit it worries me.

ALDEN. What's sending him there?

JUDITH. His work in New York was too impersonal—that's what he says. Of course there's a deeper reason too. He's never been able to adjust himself to the city.—He feels he's out of place—that's why he's lived so much within himself.—Have you noticed, Alden, he hardly ever smiles?

ALDEN. You're a little afraid of him—aren't you?

JUDITH. Times.

ALDEN. " Point number two—said the ——"

JUDITH. Don't joke about this, Alden. (*Rises.*)

ALDEN. I'm not joking—I'm probing.

JUDITH. If I married him—I could teach him —— (*We can get from her expression what she will teach him.*)

ALDEN. Have you thought *he* might do the teaching?

JUDITH. Not all ——

ALDEN. Shh! Car!

JUDITH. (*At window.*) It's he! Oh, Alden, this has got to work out!

ALDEN. Well, my pet—get him if you can, and my blessings, only remember that when an irresistible force collides with an immovable object it's—well, there's hell to pay.

JUDITH. Alden—(*She whispers it.*) let me have your rabbit's foot!

ALDEN. (*Looking in her bag hastily.*) My God, I've lost it! (*Enter* STEELE.) I've just been waiting to say hello to you, Doctor.

STEELE. Glad to see you again.

ALDEN. That's a compliment—coming from you! (*Turns to* JUDITH.) Good-bye, darling.—(*At door.*) Incidentally, Doctor, you'll get a wonderful view of Judith's brains tonight—when you see her in that new dress—'bye. (*Exit. Beyond door she turns and pulls rabbit's foot from her bag. Signals* JUDITH *and rubs it vigorously, then disappears.* JUDITH *is a little shy at first, a little breathless with eagerness and excitement.*)

JUDITH. Hello.

STEELE. Hello.—I'm not putting you out?

JUDITH. You're not putting me out.

STEELE. I like you in those things. You look fit—ready to work.

JUDITH. Sit down, Fred. Something to drink?

STEELE. Un-hunh—by and by maybe. How have you been?

JUDITH. Splendid.

STEELE. Let's have a look at you.—(*Pushes back her hair and looks at scar.*) No headache?

JUDITH. None.—You haven't been near me for three days.

STEELE. Sleeping well?

JUDITH. Beautifully.—Have you been busy?

STEELE. Very.—Appetite good?

JUDITH. Marvelous. All things according to Hoyle.

STEELE. Good. Now stand with both feet together. Close your eyes.—(*She poses elaborately.*) How's the balance?

JUDITH. Perfect. You see I know all the answers.

STEELE. I find nothing wrong.

JUDITH. There isn't anything.

STEELE. (*Smiles.*) Patient dismissed. (*Pause.*)

JUDITH. (*Thoughtfully—uneasily.*) So you're off tomorrow?

STEELE. Unless the heavens fall.

JUDITH. I have no luck with heaven.

STEELE. H'mm. I'm already a month late, Judith.

JUDITH. I didn't realize until Dr. Parsons told me that you'd given up all your plans for me. How can I ever thank you?

STEELE. Don't let's talk of thanks.

JUDITH. But I owe you—everything.

STEELE. Just seeing you as you stand there has repaid me a thousand times for anything I've done.

37

JUDITH. I'd like to believe that.

STEELE. You must. Because I don't want you ever to feel under any obligation to me.

JUDITH. I think that's the nicest thing anyone ever said to me. Are you so generous to all your patients?

STEELE. Judith—you know what I mean.

JUDITH. Perhaps I do—perhaps I don't. How much of what you mean do you ever say?

STEELE. (*Very seriously.*) Then let me say that I care so much that I'll come to you halfway across the earth, whenever you call me.—Is that better?

JUDITH. (*Vaguely disturbed at something in his tone.*) You sound awfully serious.

STEELE. It was a serious speech.

JUDITH. (*Thinking through.*) It had such—finality. (*She searches his face.*) Fred, what's disturbing you?

STEELE. Nothing.

JUDITH. Yes, there is.

STEELE. What makes you think so?

JUDITH. Why did you choose just those words—" whenever you call me "?

STEELE. I was trying to fit the rôle you picked for me.

JUDITH. You're not telling me the truth. (*Pause.*) So you're really going to be an old-fashioned country doctor?

STEELE. Hideously old-fashioned.

JUDITH. You'll get down here—occasionally?

STEELE. Not often. I expect they'll keep me pretty busy.

JUDITH. I expect so.—And you'll really love it; you'll have no regrets—not one? (*Pause.*)

STEELE. (*Goes to window, looks out. Pause.*) Judith—do you think anything worth saving was ever saved by running away from it?

JUDITH. Do you?

STEELE. I want to know what *you* think.

JUDITH. (*After pause.*) No, Fred, I don't.

STEELE. (*Turning to her.*) Do you remember the drive we took the morning of the operation, when we saw the first sun on the Palisades?

JUDITH. Yes.

STEELE. Remember what you said?

JUDITH. Tell me.

STEELE. You said that till that moment you'd never realized how magnificent they were; that it was almost as though you were seeing them for the first time with new eyes.

JUDITH. The world was very simple and clear that morning in spite of what I knew was in store for me.

STEELE. I think, *because* of it, Judith. It's apt to be that way when you know exactly what you're facing and you aren't afraid.

JUDITH. People don't show fear in front of you, Fred. They're ashamed to.

STEELE. It was a challenge, and you accepted it with perfect courage—almost with eagerness.

JUDITH. But I was glad you were beside me.

STEELE. If you knew I'd always be beside you—do you—do you think you'd ever be afraid of anything?

JUDITH. Only of one thing—of you.

STEELE. What do you mean by that, Judith?

JUDITH. How can I put it? It's the iron core in you—that unyielding something that would never let you flinch at pain, would never let you compromise with an ideal. It's what gives you your strength; but it frightens me.

STEELE. (*Troubled.*) Why?

JUDITH. Because I know I can't make any impression on it. I can't bend it—even the fraction of an inch. It's stronger than I am —it's even stronger than you.

STEELE. (*Gently.*) You mustn't be afraid.

JUDITH. You don't understand because you've never known fear, Fred.

STEELE. I've known loneliness, Judith. In fact, I've never known anything else—and that's a *kind* of fear.

JUDITH. Oh, Fred—we're getting in deep water. Before it's too late I've *got* to make you understand this: you're a very great person; I'm not. I'm shallow. You have a great purpose and a great faith—I have neither.—Believe in your work, Fred; believe in yourself—but leave me out of your belief—I'd only let you down.

STEELE. I know that isn't true.

JUDITH. I've warned you.

STEELE. I once asked you for something very important—your complete faith. Have I still got it?

39

JUDITH. (*Unable to stem the tide, swept on by it.*) You still have it.

STEELE. (*Deeply moved, takes her hand a little awkwardly.*) That means—er—that means almost everything to me ——

JUDITH. (*Softly.*) What do you mean, Fred—" almost "?

STEELE. I mean—Judith! Can't you see it? I—I want—I must have your love, dear.

JUDITH. Oh, Fred—I've wanted you to say that for so long.— Couldn't you tell?

STEELE. You see, I've never felt anything like this before. I never thought it *could* happen to me, but it has. I know now that, without you, I'm no longer anything—I'm incomplete—I'm nothing.

JUDITH. I know—in spite of all your strength, all your greatness, you've never been happy. Do you really think I can make you happy?

STEELE. (*After pause.*) We're starting on a very strange and beautiful adventure, my dear.

JUDITH. There have been millions of others in love.

STEELE. But not quite like us; none that had such need for each other (*Smiles.*) and such need for courage.

JUDITH. You make it sound so perilous, Fred.

STEELE. It is, and yet if we're sure of our love that needn't matter.

JUDITH. Are *you* sure?

STEELE. I am!

JUDITH. And yet you've never been in love before?

STEELE. (*In a higher key.*) It's a completely new experience.

JUDITH. (*Simply—naively.*) Don't you want to kiss me? (STEELE *smiles.*) Then you'd better do it.—(STEELE *kisses her simply, a little awkwardly. She laughs gaily.*) I'm afraid I'm going to have to teach you an awful lot, Fred.

STEELE. I suspect you will.

JUDITH. It'll be fun teaching you.

STEELE. It'll be fun learning.

JUDITH. Fred—I never thought! How do you take your coffee in the morning?

STEELE. Black, strong, no sugar ——

JUDITH. How utterly revolting.

STEELE. Horrible.

JUDITH. But you'll insist upon it—and upon what else? You see,

I know so little, Fred—I won't have to eat cold apple pie for breakfast—will I?

STEELE. No. Word of honor.

JUDITH. But I suppose you'll want me to entertain all your grateful patients?

STEELE. All.

JUDITH. And pay the bills on time?

STEELE. Un-hunh.

JUDITH. And run the house on a budget?

STEELE. Miss Jenny will see to that.

JUDITH. I'd forgotten about her. Your housekeeper? The one who taught you at school?

STEELE. That's the one.

JUDITH. I'm a little afraid of her.

STEELE. You'd better be!

JUDITH. Oh, Fred, I'm going to love it—every minute of it—and we'll have a garden—of course you'll want that—and babies ——? What's the matter, Fred!

STEELE. Nothing, dear—I ——

JUDITH. What's going on in your mind? What are you afraid of?

STEELE. What is there to be afraid of, if we're together?

JUDITH. (*Thoughtfully.*) Parting, I suppose.

STEELE. As I think of it, parting isn't terrible. The only terrible thing is—not to have lived.

JUDITH. Dear God, thank you for letting me be—young—and alive! (*Turning to* STEELE *with all eagerness.*) Oh, Fred, I love this earth and all the good things on it.

STEELE. (*Too solemnly.*) I'm going to help you find them, if I can.

JUDITH. (*Searching him.*) That strange solemn note whenever you talk about my future.—I've noticed —— What are you trying to keep from me?

STEELE. Nothing.

JUDITH. Don't, dear.

STEELE. You trust me?

JUDITH. You—not your words. Ever since the first day in this room I've felt that you were keeping something from me.—I've sensed it a hundred times since.

STEELE. Imagination, dear.

JUDITH. No—it's not.—All those carefully guarded phrases—

41

(*Long pause as she tries to remember them.*) " A complete *surgical recovery* "—and " I'll come to you halfway across the earth—*whenever you call me.*" (*She walks to piano and stands there quietly for a moment—thinking. Then she speaks very levelly, but quietly.*) Fred—I'm going to ask you a very simple question and I want you to answer it.—Is there anything wrong with me?

STEELE. (*Pause.*) I've told you, Judith, you may do anything you want now.

JUDITH. That won't do. I shan't let you evade this time. It has something to do with the operation.—What is it? Don't lie. You have no right to play God; no right to do that. Fred, I'm asking for the truth—and I'm entitled to it.

STEELE. You are entitled to it.—Judith, I'd hoped with all my soul this wouldn't happen, but it has—so we'll face it. (*He leads her to sofa and they sit down.*) We can now, can't we? Now, hold my hand while I tell you.—As far as surgery can go you're cured—absolutely. But there are some things surgery can't do. I shan't be technical, but when I took that thing out of your head there was a tiny part of it that couldn't be reached. It's what we call an infiltration.

JUDITH. (*Very quietly.*) So you didn't get it all out?

STEELE. All that I could see, but not quite all there was.

JUDITH. Then the operation—didn't cure me?

STEELE. It did.—This thing isn't doing you any harm—at the moment.—You see for yourself you're perfectly well.

JUDITH. For the moment.

STEELE. I'm not worried about you now—but in time—it will grow.

JUDITH. Then this horrible thing is coming back again . . . and that means another operati ——? (*She reads his face.*) No? You mean that—wouldn't do any good?—I see. Give me a cigarette, will you, please?—(*He does so and she lights it.*) Thanks—(*She draws on it deeply.*) and I'll have to face those headaches and that ghastly confusion all over again ——

STEELE. No, dear. You won't. That's all behind you. I promise you that; promise you that there'll be no suffering and no invalidism of any kind.

JUDITH. But—how will it happen?

STEELE. As quietly as going to sleep.

JUDITH. God's last small mercy! I mustn't forget to thank Him for that when I see Him!—You say I'll be perfectly well up to the —last?

STEELE. As well as you are this moment.

JUDITH. Then—how will I know! How will I know!

STEELE. Why go into all this now, Judith?

JUDITH. But I want to know if I'll have any warning—some chance to be ready?

STEELE. There will be a moment when you won't be able to—to— see as usual—that's all.

JUDITH. You mean I'll go *blind*?

STEELE. Just for a moment. Then you'll be perfectly all right again—but after a few hours, two or three—you—well, you will go to sleep.

JUDITH. (*Pause.*) I see.—How much time have I——? (*Insistently.*) How long have I before the—the end?

STEELE. Judith, dear—let that be my secret.

JUDITH. No! You've had too many secrets! . . . Go on, tell me how long?—Five years?—One year?—Six months? . . .

STEELE. Possibly more. One can't be certain—six—ten months, say.

JUDITH. That's not so very long.

STEELE. After all, time is only an illusion.

JUDITH. What does that mean?

STEELE. My dear, that we're on an adventure that can't be measured by time—because it's eternal.—Your birth was part of it, Judith; your beauty is part of it; and your death will be part of it. If you and I can reach the peak, what difference do a few hours make? What we are—the thing that's happened to us—our love— can't be revoked and can't be destroyed.

JUDITH. (*Gravely.*) You put it so eloquently—so clearly thought out —— (*Pause.*) So you knew this all along? From the very first?

STEELE. Yes.

JUDITH. And you're offering to marry me and take me to Felsboro.—(*A short dry little laugh, of despair and disillusion.*) That's very chivalrous of you, Fred—very chivalrous—so like you. (STEELE *puts his arm about her. She removes it.*) I'd rather you didn't touch me just now—do you mind?—It's still daylight—it seemed funny for a moment, that's all.

STEELE. I'd give you my own life if I could.

JUDITH. I know that, and I believe you—and I'm glad you told me.—Oh, you're so square and so strong and so unflinching—but I'm not —— (*Suddenly alert and bitter.*) God gives me something with one hand and takes it away with the other.—I was just thinking of us and the terrible difference between us—thinking how time would bring us together and now there is no time—even that has been taken away, and I can't have you. I couldn't get used to this—this thing in six months—I couldn't stand it.—I'll stay here with what I know, where I can be safe—where I can forget, for that's all I want now, just to forget and then be forgotten.

STEELE. You're coming with me to Felsboro as my wife.

JUDITH. I'm staying right here, and I'm going to live so fast and so hard that I won't be able to think.

STEELE. Where will that lead?

JUDITH. Where all roads lead in six months.—Only I haven't time to go exploring.—I'll stick to the only life I know.

STEELE. You said you loved me.

JUDITH. I didn't know what I was saying—you fooled me for a minute—but I've put the pieces all together now.—I understand—all the carefully laid preparations—how you weighed each step—planned each move—even to marrying me.—Oh, I know why you did it, and, Fred, I want you to know I'm terribly, terribly grateful.

STEELE. Why?—I love you.

JUDITH. You're only sorry for me, Fred. If you really loved me you'd have held me in your arms and comforted me; instead of that you stand there and make speeches.—It's not your fault—it's the way you're made—what you feel is pity—intellectual pity, and it's no good.—I don't want it. I want something that's alive and warm.

STEELE. Judith, you're not seeing things straight.—You can't see all the implications in this in a moment. Your world has crashed —but we're going to rebuild it together.

JUDITH. (*Covering her ears.*) I don't even hear what you're saying! I'm discovering that I'm just as hard and stubborn as you. Go away, Fred—forget about me, give yourself to your work and be happy.

STEELE. I have no life left. Don't you see that *I* need *you?* I'm

44

holding on to you because I'm no good without you.—Judith, won't you help me?

JUDITH. No, I won't. I don't want to help you—I won't accept your way of life: it's too cold, too demanding. You're like those granite hills of yours.—I admit it was generous of you, but you'd never have offered this if you hadn't known. I tell you I have no use for your pity. I don't ever want to see you again. Go to Vermont and let me die my own way. If you must think of me, then think of me as your patient. Ten years from now you can look the case up in your files: "Traherne—Judith—aged twenty-seven—diagnosis March tenth—operation March fourteenth—patient made brilliant recovery—died six months later."

STEELE. Stop it, Judith!

JUDITH. This isn't going the way you expected! Beautiful Judith Traherne isn't acting up to your sentimental picture of her. (*Pause.*) Why do you stand there and say nothing? That beautiful scientific mind judging me.—Well, what do you think of this exhibition? What do you think of me now?

STEELE. What I've always thought. I only want you to have the same faith in yourself that I have in you.

JUDITH. You've never had faith in me. *Hopes,* yes, but not faith. You thought there were too many bad spots. Oh, Fred, you're so easy for a woman to read. You despise everything I stand for in life—my set—my friends—my world. Well, thank God for that world now. My friends—will help me forget—at least they know how to be amusing, and that's all I want—it's good enough for six months ——

STEELE. It won't work, Judith, you'll never be satisfied with that. You need so much more than your friends can possibly give you.

JUDITH. He takes away my life and offers me—what? Extinction in six months. Six long months.—Oh, God, how long they seem. But don't worry—I'll fill them—I'll cram them full of living! There'll be plenty of action from now on—I'll show whoever runs this rotten world some merry hell before I've finished. You didn't know I was like this, but you've never known me—not the real me. I'm not sweet and generous. I'm a bitter, angry woman and hard—hard as nails.—Well, why do you stand there? Why don't you go? I've turned myself inside out for you—what more do you want?

STEELE. Sit down, Judith!

45

JUDITH. This isn't your office now! It's my home and I'll do in it as I like!—Please go away. My friends can lift me out of this, but you—you mean defeat, futility—death—always and always that. I mustn't ever see you again—ever.—(*Moves to phone.*) I'm calling Alden.—It's clear out and warm. I can wear my new dress.— 443 please.—My housekeeper will give you dinner.—Hello. Alden . . . Alden darling—I'm coming to the party after all—if you want me.—Oh, thanks—thanks, I'd love to—that's just what I want—a chance to celebrate and plenty to drink.—Alden, Alden, I'll be there with bells on!

CURTAIN

ACT II

Scene 2

The same. An October night. There is a moon, and the room is dimly lighted by its romantic light.

Stage empty. Bell heard consistently ringing in some distant part of the house. Voices. ALDEN *enters, followed by* JOSIE.

JOSIE. (*Turning up lights at wall switch* L. *of door.*) I'm sure she's not in, Mrs. Blaine.

ALDEN. She must be in. Where else could she be? (LESLIE CLARKE *enters.*)

CLARKE. Judith, Judith, where's my magnificent Judith!

ALDEN. Josie says she hasn't come home.

CLARKE. Not home! I must have a drink!

JOSIE. I'd have heard her come in, Mrs. Blaine.

ALDEN. You were asleep ——

JOSIE. I haven't been to bed ——

ALDEN. Leslie, what do you suppose she's done?

CLARKE. She's driving her car through the starry heavens.

ALDEN. Wrapping it round a telegraph post, you mean.

CLARKE. That's not funny, Alden.

ALDEN. Nothing she's been doing for the past three months is funny.

46

JOSIE. I'll look in her room.—I hope there's nothing the matter, Mrs. Blaine.

ALDEN. Don't stand there talking. Go on up and see.

CLARKE. Leave her alone and she'll come home —— (*Goes to piano.*)

ALDEN. (*Crosses to L. of piano.*) A swell woolly white lamb she turned out to be.—Where in hell could she have gone?

CLARKE. Gone to Heaven to tell St. Peter the joke. (*He starts to play. Interrupting himself.*) The first woman to enter Heaven on a horse ——

ALDEN. You're going to be a great help in this situation.

CLARKE. I'll get her back to the club—she'll listen to me—I'll learn the gal to ——

ALDEN. You learn to hold your liquor! (*Sits R. C.*)

CLARKE. Yes, I'm drunk, but I'm drunk with adoration. For Judith. Judith, the Valkyrie, Judith this afternoon carrying off her silver cups and ribbons—Judith tonight with those dark eyes blazing in that white face ——

ALDEN. God knows it was white!

CLARKE. Moon-white! Moon-mad!

ALDEN. (*Rises—crosses up L. C.*) Just right for a formal dinner.

CLARKE. We're not good enough for her. What am I, a stockbroker—what is she, a pagan?

ALDEN. You talk like one of my lousy books.

CLARKE. She's met Pan by the river.

ALDEN. (*Sits chair below sofa.*) Unfortunately Pan isn't in the Social Register any more.

CLARKE. Alack, you are so right! Pan, Pan is dead —— (*With musical accompaniment.*)

> " Gods of Hellas, gods of Hellas,
> Can ye listen in your silence?
> Pan, Pan is dead."

(*He breaks into jazz.*) But I got rhythm, I got rhythm! (*JOSIE enters—crosses to ALDEN.*)

JOSIE. She isn't in, Mrs. Blaine. I've looked everywhere.—Oh, I do hope nothing's wrong.

CLARKE. Look at the girl—frightened! Laugh, girl, laugh! (*He rises.*) A Gargantuan joke has been perpetrated tonight. Your magnificent mistress has cut her name in the left breast of the Muse of History. " A toast to Judith Traherne," cries the dinner committee, " many cups and a long life ——" " Many cups and a long life," cries the stewed but patrician gathering —— (*He has left piano and is filling a glass with whiskey which he now holds aloft.*) Up goes her glass. " Long life to Judith Traherne," she cries, looking like the Avenging Angel and with that—wham goes her glass—(ALDEN *rises, crosses up—sits on sofa.*) and she walks out—(*Imitates her walk.*) just like that. (*Crosses to piano—starts jazz number.* JUDITH *enters.* CLARKE *rises and goes to her.*) Judith! Judith! My adorable Judith!

JUDITH. Oh, go away, Leslie—let me alone. (CLARKE *goes back to piano—starts to play. He hits piano.*)

CLARKE. Okay, lady.

JUDITH. (*To* JOSIE.) You can go back to bed. (JOSIE *goes.*) Thanks for being here, Alden. I thought I was washed up with all of you.

ALDEN. I've partially squared it for you—but you'll have to do the rest.

JUDITH. I'm not going back to the club, Alden.

ALDEN. A little soft soap to your host and an apology to that old bitch, Mrs. Conway, for the mess you made of her gown are very much in order.

JUDITH. I won't apologize. Not to those people.

ALDEN. For God's sake, girl —— (*Rises.*)

JUDITH. Those damned, empty, smug faces, not even amusingly drunk ——

ALDEN. (*Crosses to* JUDITH.) You haven't got that excuse. You were cold sober all evening.

JUDITH. I was afraid to drink. I was afraid I'd let go tonight.

ALDEN. My God, you couldn't have done anything worse than you did.

JUDITH. (*Trying to stop her. Sits bench* R. C.) I know, I know, I know. You don't have to tell me.

ALDEN. Someone's got to tell you. How long do you think you can go on this way—you've been raising Hell for months.—You could fill the Yale Bowl with the people who are sore at you.

CLARKE. Let 'em be sore at her. She's got me, the son of that old crook, Judge Roger Clarke, to protect her.

JUDITH. Leslie, for God's sake!

CLARKE. A little softer, all right, a little softer —— (*Plays something sentimental.*)

JUDITH. Pretty soon I won't be a problem to you, Alden—pretty soon ——

ALDEN. I hope you've been having a better time than you seemed to be having.

CLARKE. She's had a glorious time—she's been on more and bigger binges than anyone in six counties.

ALDEN. Even in this best of all possible civilizations women still get annoyed if other women cop their husbands or lovers. (JUDITH *rises, crosses to table* L. *of piano. Mixes highball.*) I'm not suggesting that you slept with them—I hope not all of them at any rate.

JUDITH. Shall I send them flowers, Alden?

ALDEN. I won't have them drop you. You're a devil but I love you —I won't have you hurt.

JUDITH. That's so funny, Alden.

ALDEN. If you could only hear what they're saying about you.

JUDITH. Let them wait till I'm dead to pick my bones.

ALDEN. That's right, fight me off! It's what you do with everyone who tries to be decent to you.

JUDITH. Alden, I'd let you help me if there was anything you could do for me.

ALDEN. Oh, Judith, are you still eating your heart out about Steele?

JUDITH. Oh—you mean that extraordinary surgeon ——

ALDEN. (*Ignoring her flippancy.*) I knew something went wrong there.

JUDITH. All according to plan. He planned for Vermont, he went to Vermont.

ALDEN. Why didn't you go after him?

JUDITH. Vermont's a long way off and it's cold when you get there. (*Puts highball glass on end table.*)

ALDEN. Well, then forget him.

JUDITH. He was a wicked man, Alden.—He took me to a high place and showed me the kingdoms of the earth.—God, Alden, never do that to anyone.—Don't show them what they can't have.

CLARKE. I got rhythm—I got rhythm.

JUDITH. Shut up! (*She sits on sofa.*)

ALDEN. Leslie, for God's sake! (*To* JUDITH.) The way we both feel—we'd better go on a binge tonight.

JUDITH. You can't make a binge last forever.

ALDEN. Don't get philosophical—that's my job—put on your coat.

CLARKE. All coats on—all coats on! (*Rises—crosses* R. *around piano.*)

JUDITH. Stay here with me, Alden.

ALDEN. Two neurotic females watching the sun come up—no, thank you.

JUDITH. I can't bear being alone ——

ALDEN. Darling, the club's full of lads who'd be glad to take care of that.

CLARKE. Yeah—go back to the club—and give 'em the other barrel. —Do it all over again.—Many cups and a long life —— (*Picks up cup and brandishes it.*) Many cups and a long life —— Wheeee! (*Flings it through window* R. *A smash of glass, then silence.*)

JUDITH. Oh! (*Covers face with her hands.*)

ALDEN. It's all right, darling ——

JUDITH. You inconsiderate fool!

ALDEN. Leslie, I could murder you ——

JUDITH. Why did you come here—why did either of you come? Why can't you leave me alone? (*Crosses to fireplace.*)

ALDEN. Leslie, go on out to the car.

CLARKE. Let me stay. I won't do it again.

ALDEN. Oh, use your head and go. (*Crosses to* JUDITH.) Judith, I've been frightfully tactless about this. I didn't realize how upset you were.

JUDITH. I'm a fool to go to pieces like that.

ALDEN. (*Back of sofa.*) I don't blame you. Now if you'd like me to stay here ——

JUDITH. What's the good of our sitting here like two stone images? (*Enter* MICHAEL *and* JOSIE. JOSIE *up* C.—MICHAEL R. *of piano.*)

JOSIE. What is it, Miss Traherne?

MICHAEL. We heard glass.

ALDEN. Nothing, just a broken window.

JUDITH. Go on back to bed, Josie. (JOSIE *hesitates.* JUDITH *sits on back of sofa.*) I'm coming, Alden. If they want my company they can have it—what's left of it after Leslie's performance. Headlines for the tabloids—Cup-Winner Crawls Back.

ALDEN. Now, if you want to wait a few minutes ——

JUDITH. Do I look as shot as all that?

ALDEN. Oh, don't be an idiot.

JUDITH. You go on with Leslie while I recondition my beautiful face.—I'll be right along.

ALDEN. Right, and I'll see that Leslie is kept in the cloak room. (*Crosses to* CLARKE.)

CLARKE. Bring out the fatted calf, she's on her way—I've got rhythm—I've got rhythm. (*Exit* CLARKE *and* ALDEN.)

MICHAEL. (*Picks up cup.* R. *of piano.*) A fine mess they've made of our cup!

JUDITH. (*Rises.*) Hurrah for the cup! (JOSIE *crosses to* JUDITH *with coat.*)

JOSIE. Will you put on your coat now, miss?

JUDITH. Yes. (JUDITH *puts coat on, walks slowly toward door, decides against going, crosses* L. *to sofa.* JUDITH *sits sofa.* JOSIE *crosses* L. *to end table by sofa.*)

JOSIE. You're not going back to the club?

JUDITH. I must go back. I just want a minute.

JOSIE. Then let me get you a cup of coffee.

JUDITH. No, don't leave me alone, Josie ——

JOSIE. I'll only be a minute. Michael will stay.

JUDITH. All right. Coffee.—(JOSIE *goes. Pause.*) Michael, talk to me.

MICHAEL. Yes, Miss Judith.

JUDITH. Go on.

MICHAEL. What shall I talk about, Miss Judith?

JUDITH. Anything. Just talk.

MICHAEL. It was a grand show this afternoon.

JUDITH. Was it?

MICHAEL. And you the best one in it.

JUDITH. H'm!

MICHAEL. You've been goin' too hard, Miss Judith, you've got yourself tired out. I know you've got to have action in your life the way I've got to have action in mine. We live only once ——

JUDITH. Only once.

MICHAEL. But no one can go on as you've been goin'! Ridin', swimmin', dancin'. Goin' day and night. You can't do that and keep on with your jumpin' horses. The glorious jumpin' you did at the show this afternoon you did on your nerve. Ye had me heart in me mouth a dozen times. That was terrible hard ye were drivin' yourself for a cup ye didn't want.

JUDITH. I did want it. (*Throws off coat—goes to fireplace.*)

51

MICHAEL. Sure, for the winnin' of it, that's all. It's the fightin' that counts with you. But you'll win no more cups, Miss Judith, the way you're goin'—and think of the shame to me if you don't. All I can do is to get the horses ready—it's you that does the ridin'.

JUDITH. Is it hard being a groom, Michael?

MICHAEL. It's hell at times. The thoughts you have to smother down.

JUDITH. Forget you're a groom, Michael, and talk to me as a man.

MICHAEL. (*Dangerously*.) You're takin' a chance sayin' that to me.

JUDITH. I like taking chances!

MICHAEL. What is it you want to know?

JUDITH. About you, and the thoughts you have to smother down.

MICHAEL. Well, my father was an actor and he wanted to get into the Abbey Theater, but he was a drunken loafer with a breath you could smell across the half of Ireland. But he was a man, and he had poetry in him; and he brought me up on the stories of the heroes and heroines of old Ireland—and that's where me thoughts come in.

JUDITH. Go on, Michael.

MICHAEL. I was born out of me time, Miss Judith.

JUDITH. It doesn't matter when you're born, Michael.

MICHAEL. You're wrong about that. I should have lived in the days when it counted to be a man—the way I can ride and the way I can fight. What's ridin' and havin' an arm like iron and an eye like a hawk get you today? Do ye begin to see me thoughts?

JUDITH. I'm not sure.

MICHAEL. Then I'll tell ye. If I'd have lived in the olden days, I'd be no one's groom. They'd have taken me for what I am—a man! I'd have had fine women in them days—women like you, Miss Judith.

JUDITH. You can leave me out of it.

MICHAEL. You invited me to talk to you, and it's as a man I'm talkin'. A thousand times a better man than them creatures that's playin' around with you. They're afraid of ye. I hear 'em talkin' when I'm holdin' the horses—how they'd go after ye but for the fear of ye that's in them. By God, if I was in their boots, I'd quiet the restlessness that's drivin' ye like an imp of Satan—I'd make you stop needin' to risk your lovely white column of a neck for a lousy silver cup! By God, the nights I've laid awake wantin' ye and the great beauty of ye ——

JUDITH. Do you realize you're making love to me?

MICHAEL. I've loved ye since the first day I set foot in your house.

JUDITH. Don't say that to me!

MICHAEL. I'll say what I want to ye!—for you're down to my level now—and I know it.

JUDITH. Michael!

MICHAEL. And ye can't deny it for I've watched it happen day by day. You still have a fighting heart, Miss Judith, but your quality's gone.

JUDITH. Don't say that!

MICHAEL. A blind man could see it. If it wasn't for Mrs. Blaine ye wouldn't have a friend left, ye'd be down to scum like that thing that was in here tonight—and even they're laughin' at ye and gossipin' about ye.

JUDITH. Indeed! How tragic!

MICHAEL. Look in the glass if ye don't believe it—why, you're like —I don't know what you're like—like that cup there, bent and tarnished! You've lost caste. Do ye think I'd have dared talk to ye this way if ye hadn't? When I came here first, by God! you were queen of the world—tho' I loved ye, I knew ye were above me. But I was proud to work for ye, tho' it near killed me not to be able to say what was in me heart.—I loved ye then as a queen, but I'll love ye now—as a groom. (*Enter* JOSIE *with coffee.*)

JOSIE. Here's your coffee, miss.

JUDITH. Put it over there, Josie. Go to bed. (JOSIE *puts coffee tray on table. Exits.* JUDITH, *after long pause.*) Thanks for telling me the truth, but it's only part of the truth. If you knew it all, you wouldn't want me—even that way. No man could. (*Another pause.*) God! I can't die like this!

MICHAEL. Die? What's this crazy talk of dyin'?

JUDITH. I'm going to die, Michael, in about two months. (*He stares at her.*) It's this thing in my brain. It's coming back—and it's going to kill me. Dr. Steele said so.

MICHAEL. God in heaven, Miss Judith!

JUDITH. You'd have held a dead woman in your arms tonight, if I'd let you. Does that frighten you? It is rather repulsive—isn't it?

MICHAEL. Don't ye know ye can be damned to hell for sayin' less than that!

JUDITH. I can't—I've been there. The time that's run to waste—hours, days, weeks—gone! Nothing to show! Profitless, sterile. Oh, it's all been so cheap and undignified—and so damned stupid!

MICHAEL. This is a terrible road ye've been travelling. God forgive me for all I've said. I didn't know.

JUDITH. It's not so hard to die, Michael, I've faced that. It's dying without having lived. . . . (*Pause—to herself.*) I—I ——

MICHAEL. What, Miss Judith?

JUDITH. I'm going away tomorrow.

MICHAEL. Leaving tomorrow? I'd heard no word.

JUDITH. I'm deciding now.

MICHAEL. Wherever it is, Miss Judith—I'll wish ye luck.

JUDITH. Thanks, Michael, I'll need it. (*Goes to window* R., *looks out.*) Don't worry about me. I'm all right. (MICHAEL *hesitates uncertainly.*) The stars are so bright, aren't they?

MICHAEL. It's been a grand autumn with the color.

JUDITH. The geese were going south, today.

MICHAEL. The old year puts up a fine show just at the last.

JUDITH. It knows how to die—beautifully.—Good-bye, Michael.

MICHAEL. Good-bye. (*He goes.*)

JUDITH. (*Still looking out window, very quietly.*) Fred—I'm coming.

CURTAIN

ACT III

SCENE 1

Living-room of STEELE'S *house in Felsboro.*
TIME: *Evening of the next day.*

It is definitely a man's room. Comfortable—though perhaps on the bare side. Rear is front door opening on a gravel path, which leads to road. Close to corner, L., is STEELE'S *desk and set in corner are triangular shelves which serve him as a home laboratory, bottles, tubes, etc., on them. Directly down from shelves is a table with an instrument sterilizer upon it. R. C. an open fire, burning, and before it a sofa. Small table by sofa, on which is a tray with milk and sandwiches. L. a door which leads to hall.*

AT RISE: STEELE *enters—closes door—puts bag on desk* L. *Puts instruments in sterilizer. Takes off coat and hat, puts them on chair* R. *of door. Warms himself at fire* R. *Sits sofa* R. *A glance at his desk, then sits down to his supper. He has changed since we last saw him. He appears even to have aged somewhat. In any case, his face is somber enough as we see him at supper. Enter* MISS JENNY L. *A fine New Englander of sixty, tall, erect and slender. White hair done in the fashion of 1905. A fine nose and a firm mouth and chin. Reserved, dignified and critical.* STEELE *looks up, hearing her. She brings in a plate of food.*

STEELE. Hello, Miss Jenny. (*Sits on sofa.*)
JENNY. You're late tonight, Dr. Fred.
STEELE. I had to stay at the Frasers' longer than I expected.
JENNY. It's after nine. (*Puts plate of food on table below sofa.*)
STEELE. I know. I saw the train pull out as I came by the station!
JENNY. This is the *third* night you have been late.

STEELE. From now on, Miss Jenny, I am at your service—as always.

JENNY. From now on, Dr. Fred, (*Puts cushion behind him.*) you're to be home every night for a hot supper. You can't live on just bread and milk.

STEELE. Point one; bread and milk is a perfect food. Point two; a doctor's time is not his own. (MISS JENNY *shakes her head—she has heard this before.*) And point three—you're an awful bully. Now what do you know about *that?*

JENNY. I know from long experience, Frederick, that the time to break a habit is before it becomes a habit. (MISS JENNY *crosses to desk—gets his pipe and tobacco pouch.*)

STEELE. Miss Jenny, every time I hear that note in your voice, I'm right back in the schoolroom expecting that inevitable " Frederick Steele will remain after school is dismissed! " Brrgh! Gives me a chill just to think of.

JENNY. Were the punishments as bad as that?

STEELE. It wasn't the punishments, Miss Jenny; it was your cold, disapproving eye. Great mistake ever to have you keep house for me. But it is pleasant to sit here with just you.

JENNY. (*She sits in chair down* R. *of fireplace.*) You're tired tonight.

STEELE. I hadn't thought. Maybe I am.

JENNY. I don't like your looking so tired.

STEELE. You haven't changed any, have you?

JENNY. *You* have.

STEELE. Now don't worry about me, Miss Jenny. I'm not in the second grade any longer.

JENNY. A lot of water's gone under the bridge since then, Frederick. (*She rises—settles cushion behind his back—then sits on sofa—*R. *of* STEELE.)

STEELE. Lord, yes. Mother and Dad —— Sister married and living in London. But I always knew I'd come back. I'm where I belong—at last. (*Lights his pipe.*)

JENNY. *Are* you, Dr. Fred?

STEELE. I have everything I need now. I'm home, and doing what I've always wanted to do.

JENNY. Sometimes I think life here is on a pretty small scale.

STEELE. That's because you have something to measure it against —the hills.

JENNY. Perhaps it's just an old woman's fancy. You see, I've never been away very much.

STEELE. I have, (*Rises—crosses up* C.) and I didn't find life any bigger—just a lot noisier and more confused—that's all.

JENNY. (*Rises—arranges plates, etc., on tray.*) Then you didn't find the Garden of the Hesperides in your travels?

STEELE. (*To door* C.) I'm not even sure that it exists, Miss Jenny —— (*He looks out small window* L. *of door.*) They've gone.

JENNY. What is it?

STEELE. Nothing. I thought I heard someone, that's all. I thought I recognized the step.

JENNY. Are you expecting someone? (*Crosses* L. *to desk with tray.*)

STEELE. No, Miss Jenny. (*He moves down* L.)

JENNY. (*Puts tray on desk.*) Oh, Frederick, what has hurt you so?

STEELE. You're imagining things. (*Sits in chair below desk.*)

JENNY. No, I'm not.

STEELE. There's nothing the matter with me.

JENNY. There's something haunting you, and you'll never be happy until that ghost is laid.

STEELE. Ghosts die, Miss Jenny, like anything else. (*Glances at his appointment book.*)

JENNY. Are you sure?

STEELE. Quite sure.

JENNY. I wish you were contented, Frederick.

STEELE. Nothing is ever complete. There's no such thing as perfection, I've learned that.

JENNY. You didn't used to think so.

STEELE. But I've learned. You see, I came very close to it once. To the thing itself! I held it in my hand. And then—I lost it. (*Rises.*) God!—Why are we New Englanders as we are?

JENNY. I'm sorry.

STEELE. Quite all right, Miss Jenny. I've just put in a rather bad hour with Ruth Fraser, that's all. Big Ruth, I mean.

JENNY. (*Behind desk.*) Is the child worse?

STEELE. No, she's going to get well.

JENNY. Surely, then ——

STEELE. Ruth rather went to pieces when I told her. (*Lights pipe*

57

again.) Just reaction. People do that when the tension is broken.

JENNY. That's perfectly natural.

STEELE. Yes. But I don't think there's anything more terrible, really, than to see a fine woman suddenly crack. You see the hurt, frightened animal underneath, and you realize how thin the layer is. But she's all right now. I gave her morphine before I left. She'll sleep well tonight. (STEELE *crosses up* C. *by door.* MISS JENNY *starts out* L.) I hope all my patients sleep well tonight.

JENNY. (*Stops at door.*) If you stay up, you'd best put another log on the fire. It's none too warm.

STEELE. All right.

JENNY. Good night, Dr. Fred.

STEELE. Good night, Miss Jenny. (*She goes out.* STEELE *picks up a book and reads. A knock at door of vestibule.*) Come in. (*Puts pipe on mantel. A second knock at inner door. Putting log on fire.*) Come in! (JUDITH *enters.* STEELE *crosses to her quickly.*) Judith!

JUDITH. Yes, I've come. (*Drops her suitcase.*) I'm sorry.

STEELE. Judith —— Steady!

JUDITH. Oh, I'm all right. (*He closes door.*)

STEELE. Your eyes. They're all right?

JUDITH. Yes.

STEELE. Can I believe you?

JUDITH. You can believe me—now.

STEELE. Thank God! (JUDITH *crosses to sofa* R.—*sits down.*) Steady!

JUDITH. It's the sudden warmth.

STEELE. (*Sits beside her* L. *end of sofa.*) Of course you're all right. It's nothing. Just done up a bit, that's all. We're going to get you warmed up now. (*Feeling her hand.*) Lord! You're half frozen. (*He goes to cabinet* U. R., *takes bottle of whiskey and glass.*) Well, we'll fix that in. no time. (*She removes her hat and coat.*) Get some of this inside you, and you'll feel better. Here. Drink this. `

JUDITH. No—no, thanks.

STEELE. Do as I say. (JUDITH *drinks.*) That's better, isn't it? (*Puts glass and bottle on mantel* R.) You'll feel like a fighting cock in a minute. Wait! I'll stir this up. (*Crosses to fireplace above sofa. Pokes fire, then to* R. *of* JUDITH *on sofa.*) Judith—how did you get here?

JUDITH. Walked.

STEELE. All the way from the station?

JUDITH. There wasn't a taxi.

STEELE. How did you find the house?

JUDITH. I missed it the first time. Then I came back.

STEELE. Better now?

JUDITH. Yes. Fred, I must talk to you.

STEELE. Not tonight. Tomorrow.

JUDITH. I've come to tell you something very important, and I've come a long way. You'd better hear me now.

STEELE. (*Sits sofa, R. of her.*) All right—go on.

JUDITH. How comfortable it is here.—Fred, I've done what I said I would.

STEELE. I thought you would.

JUDITH. Everything—to the last empty boast.

STEELE. Why do you tell me all this?

JUDITH. Because I couldn't die knowing your bitterness toward me—you mustn't think of me like that. Please don't, darling. How good it is to call you that. I couldn't bear to have you go on feeling that way forever.

STEELE. Stop it, Judith. Do you think you're the only one who has discovered anything? Do you think I have found happiness in this empty house? I should have taken you with me—but never have told you a word.

JUDITH. It wouldn't have worked. I wasn't ready.

STEELE. Judith, I failed you.

JUDITH. I failed myself. I found that out at last—so I've come. I won't demand much—your strength will help me face myself.

STEELE. I can give you so much more than that.

JUDITH. I don't want more. I wouldn't know what to do with it, now. I'm pretty spent, Fred—inside me.

STEELE. I love you, Juidth. . . . (*Takes her in his arms.*) I'm never going to let you go again.

JUDITH. A man and a dying girl have met to love.—(*Suddenly frightened.*) Oh, Fred, it's too late!

STEELE. (*Holding her closer.*) No!

JUDITH. How can you—with what we know?

STEELE. We're together—now.

JUDITH. For a moment.

STEELE. Always.

JUDITH. Darling, a moment isn't forever.

STEELE. That's all that lovers ever have. A few perfect hours. I tried to explain that to you—before.

JUDITH. What will this do to you? A shadow's fallen on my earth. It mustn't fall on yours.

STEELE. It's been falling since time began, my darling. Listen! Between now—and now—there's been birth and the passing of life, sunset and dawn—and your shadow's mine, and your victory over it—that's mine too.

JUDITH. Then I must never interfere with your work—you must promise me that. It must be part of our bargain if we're to be together now.

STEELE. You're going to help me. It's through you that I'm going to be the kind of doctor I've always wanted to be.

JUDITH. I want to help you—I must give you something of me that will live on in your work, after I've gone. When I've done that, what more could I possibly do?

STEELE. You're the only person who can give me that. (*She relaxes completely in his arms. Long pause.*)

JUDITH. Must tomorrow come?

STEELE. Darling—let it come! (*He holds her close.*)

CURTAIN

ACT III

SCENE 2

Same. Tea table in front of sofa.

TIME: *Afternoon in late January, two months later.*
The room has softened in appearance since last we saw it. New and bright curtains have been hung in windows, some comfortable chairs have been added, and there are green things about: ivy in pots, fruit sprays and forsythia that have been forced. The whole tone of the room is gay. Through the windows intense winter sunlight pours in.

AT RISE: JUDITH *is sitting at desk, busy at accounts.* MISS JENNY *enters from* L. *She carries a plate of cake which she puts on tea table below sofa* R.

JUDITH. We have a deficit for the month, Miss Jenny—forty-three dollars and seventeen cents.

JENNY. (R. *of sofa.*) That's splendid, Mrs. Fred. It was over a hundred last month.

JUDITH. At this rate, we'll soon be living within our income.

JENNY. Don't tell your husband or he won't even mail his bills.

JUDITH. Miss Jenny, who *did* collect the bills before I came?

JENNY. (*Puts cake on table* R.) The patients collected them.

JUDITH. And still doing it, some of them. Here's John Hunter with a bill of eight dollars sent four months ago.

JENNY. My dear, if John Hunter ever paid a bill, the whole county would rock on its foundations.

JUDITH. I know. And he's such a kind man. (*Throwing paper away.*) He looks just like a horse.

JENNY. (*She crosses up to behind table* R.) He's mule through and through.

JUDITH. Oh dear! And the Ralph Cummings owe us twenty dollars for a baby. And the Joe Harrises twenty-five for twins.

JENNY. H'mmm. Only five dollars difference?

JUDITH. Isn't that the law of diminishing returns? Oh, good Lord!

JENNY. What is it?

JUDITH. I forgot to take those books to Mrs. Waring. She asked Fred for "David Copperfield" and a detective story. (*Up.*) Where'll I find the Dickens set?

JENNY. On the third shelf in the guest-room. It's bound in red. (MISS JENNY *crosses over to door* L. *Exit* JUDITH L. MISS JENNY *returns to finish her work.* POSTMAN'S *whistle is heard at front door.* MISS JENNY *opens it.*)

POSTMAN. Got a big parcel for you.

JENNY. I see. (*She puts parcel on chair* L. *of door.*)

POSTMAN. You'll have to sign for it.

JENNY. I suppose so. (*Signing.*) There—thank you.

POSTMAN. Gettin' pretty cold, ain't it?

JENNY. Yes—shut the door when you go out! (*She takes letters to desk* L. *Then picks up package and takes it to table* R. *behind sofa. Re-enter* JUDITH. *Sees package.*)

JUDITH. (*Puts book on desk—goes through mail—none of it important—throws it down.*) Oh! They've come! Open them, Miss Jenny.

JENNY. They appear to have—but what?

JUDITH. The bulbs, silly. Dutch bulbs. Holland to Felsboro, via Macy's.

JENNY. A very small country to produce so many bulbs.

JUDITH. I hope they haven't left any out.

JENNY. I don't believe they have left any *out!*

JUDITH. *(Inspecting forsythia and potted plants at window U. L.)* See, Miss Jenny, they've opened since lunch. It's that marvelous sunshine. Aren't they sweet?

JENNY. *(She has opened outside cardboard box, and is removing smaller boxes from within. Each is labeled and she reads.)* Poeticus; Incomparabilis; Cyclaminous; Jonquilla; Narcissus; Rugulosis.

JUDITH. *(Takes one box—examines bulbs, sits on sofa.)* Of the ancient and honorable Narcissus family of Rome.

JENNY. What a pretty name. Jonquilla Narcissus.

JUDITH. The Hon. Senator and Mrs. Narcissus request the pleasure of your company at a gladiatorial combat given in honor of their debutante daughter " Jonquilla " in the forum at eight o'clock. Fireworks from the Janiculum at nine.

JENNY. Idiot!

JUDITH. We'll start them today, Miss Jenny. Of course they won't bloom till late spring now.

JENNY. Happy?

JUDITH. Terribly!

JENNY. A two months' bride should be.

JUDITH. Please. Don't speak of the months.

JENNY. Very well.

(Phone rings. JUDITH crosses to desk, sits.)

JUDITH. Long distance. I can tell by the ring. Hello? Yes. Montreal is calling Dr. Steele? No. He isn't. *(MISS JENNY gets box of bulbs JUDITH left on sofa. Puts them on table back of sofa. Leaves box open.)* I see. An emergency call from Dr. Platt. Just a moment now. *(Looks at memo pad.)* Hello. You may be able to reach him at Felsboro 93. But he's probably on his way home now. Yes. But if you can't reach him at 93, and he doesn't get through to you within five minutes, call me back and I'll get hold of him somehow. That's right. *(Hangs up.)* Emergency call. I don't like that. Miss Jenny, they wouldn't call him to Montreal?

JENNY. *(Crosses L. C.)* It's possible. Now don't worry, Mrs. Fred; even if he had to go, he'd soon be back.

JUDITH. Yes.

JENNY. You mustn't fret every time he goes out of the house.

JUDITH. I know. I can't help grudging every minute he's away, every second.

JENNY. You shouldn't have married a doctor.

JUDITH. Oh, please don't say that.

JENNY. (*Crosses to* L. C.) I didn't mean it, silly.

JUDITH. Miss Jenny?

JENNY. Yes?

JUDITH. You—you'll always look after Fred—I mean Fred and me, of course—won't you?

JENNY. If you want.

JUDITH. Oh, I do, I do! (*Rises.*) Only I want you to promise!

JENNY. I'll promise anything you want. (*Up* C.)

JUDITH. (*Crosses* R.) Miss Jenny, what was he like when he was a little boy? Nasty?

JENNY. (*At desk—moves phone downstage on desk.*) All little boys are nasty!

JUDITH. Oh, he wasn't!

JENNY. Very well, just as you wish.

JUDITH. No, but tell me, Miss Jenny! You see I know nothing about his family. Was he happy? Did they love him?

JENNY. They weren't a demonstrative family. (*Follows* JUDITH R.) But they were fond of each other and they respected one another.

JUDITH. Respect and fondness. That's it.

JENNY. Well, he has everything now. (*Crosses to desk, puts ledger in drawer, straightens papers, etc.*)

JUDITH. (*At window* R. *Pause. Looks up at sky.*) I wish it wouldn't cloud up like this.

JENNY. What are you talking about?

JUDITH. I don't like its getting overcast so suddenly. It means a storm.

JENNY. (*Looks out* U. L. *window.*) But the sun's out! (*To* U. R. C.) I never saw it brighter.

JUDITH. But it's getting—dimmer—each second —— Look! (*Holds her hands up to light, turning them slowly.*) Curious how I can still feel the heat of it.

JENNY. Mrs. Fred! (*Crosses* R. *two paces.*)

JUDITH (*Turns facing room.*) Why—how dark it's gotten! (*Suddenly* JUDITH'S *hand goes to her throat. There is an intake of breath.*) Agh! (*Terror, hands over eyes.*) Miss Jenny!

(MISS JENNY *moves further* R.)

JENNY (*Close to her.*) What is it, dear?

JUDITH. N-nothing. (*She laughs; tries to make it sound natural, but cannot.*) Nothing! Nothing! Don't you see? (*Laughs again, more convincingly this time.*) Don't pay any attention to me. You can't understand. You're just an old maid, you dear! (*She is laughing again, then suddenly phone rings sharply.*) Long distance again. I'll answer! (*She is near desk, and though she is almost blind, she feels her way there without too much show of awkwardness. But once seated, she cannot find the instrument. She gropes for it as it rings again.*) Miss Jenny! Give it to me! Give it to me! (*Sits at desk—*MISS JENNY *at her* L.) Hello? Yes. Oh, you couldn't get him at 93? No, he hasn't come. This is Mrs. Steele speaking. Could I take the message? No? All right. Tell Dr. Platt that I'll get him somehow. Right. Good-bye. (*During conversation,* JUDITH *has, as it were, looked around room testing her eyes. She now hangs up, accurately replaces receiver on hook. Her vision has returned, though blurred, and she has had time in which to recover herself a little.*)

JENNY. (L. *of* JUDITH.) Mrs. Fred!

JUDITH. Miss Jenny—don't worry about me—I'm all right. I think I hear a car! See if it's Fred!

JENNY. (*To* U. L. *window.*) It is!

JUDITH. (*Rises, takes books.*) I'll be right back. I'll take these books to Mrs. Waring. (*Crosses* L. *door.*) Then I'll come back and pack Fred's things.

JENNY. (R. *of her.*) Let me do it, Mrs. Fred!

JUDITH. You stay here. Tell Fred to call the Montreal operator. I'll go the back way. It's shorter. (*To door* L.) Miss Jenny, say nothing to him about—about anything —— Promise? (*Exit* JUDITH L.)

(MISS JENNY *follows to door.* STEELE *enters.*)

STEELE. (*Puts bag on chair* R. *of door.*) Hello, Miss Jenny. Where's Judith?

JENNY. (*Above desk.*) She's just stepped over to Mrs. Waring's—she'll be right back.

STEELE. Everything all right?

JENNY. Of course.

STEELE. Yes, of course.

JENNY. Montreal has been trying to get you.

STEELE. Montreal?! (*Puts coat and bat on chair R. of door.*)

JENNY. (L. *of chair behind desk.*) They've called twice.

STEELE. Who was it?

JENNY. You're to call the operator at once.

STEELE. What do they want?

JENNY. An emergency call. (STEELE *goes to table behind sofa. Picks up bulb from small box, examines it carefully. Long pause.*) You'd better put that call in, Dr. Fred. (*Gestures toward phone.*)

STEELE. One minute, Miss Jenny! Don't be in such a hurry. It's probably nothing important. (*Crosses to C.*) I'm tired. It's been a busy day. Isn't this room marvelous with all these flowers?

JENNY. (L. *end of desk.*) They do better for certain people.

STEELE. Yes. (R. C.) It's that way with everything she touches.

JENNY. Dr. Fred! (*Indicates phone again.*)

STEELE. Oh, all right! (*Slowly crosses and sits at desk. Picks up phone.*) Hello! Dr. Steele speaking. I was to call the Montreal operator. Right, I'll wait. Yes, it's a different place now, with Judith.

JENNY. It's been such a short time, I can hardly remember what it was like without her. (*At L. of desk.*)

STEELE. Can't you?—I'm glad you approve my choice of brides, Miss Jenny.

JENNY. If ever I had a son, Dr. Fred, I could want no more for him.

STEELE. You are a dear, (*Takes her hand.*) Miss Jenny, and you are right, too.

JENNY. And she's learning to be a very good cook.

STEELE. Yes. But just between you and me, I think she's a —— Oh, hello. (*Talks in phone.* MISS JENNY *exits D. L.*) Hello. Yes, put Dr. Platt on, will you? Hello, hello, Stephen. Yes. Did you want me? Skidded off the bridge? Phew. Fractured skull, you say. What are the chances? I see. Stephen, I—(JUDITH *enters—L. 1. Goes up toward window L.*) don't see how I can. Yes, but it means at least three days! No, no one very sick at the moment, but anything might happen. No, not from what you say. No chance unless you operate. Yes, it is delicate. Yes, I've had good results. Off-hand I don't know anyone else who has—I know— but really, Stephen, there must be someone in Montreal. Yes, I see that, but even so I—I don't ——

JUDITH. (*Crossing down to desk, covering mouthpiece with her hand.*) You must.

STEELE. But, darling, it means at least three days.

JUDITH. But you must.

STEELE. (*In phone.*) Hold on, Stephen. Hold it.

JUDITH. (*With gentleness, but authority.*) My dearest, this is your work, your life, this comes first.

STEELE. But, Judith—someone else can do the operation.

JUDITH. (*Smiling.*) The land is full of great brain specialists, isn't it? All of them better than Frederick Steele?

STEELE. But you, darling? You're—you feel perfectly well, do you?

JUDITH. What more can you ask? Don't I look perfect?

STEELE. (*In phone.*) One second. (JUDITH *lays an arm on his shoulder and* STEELE *again speaks into phone.*) Well, how about trains, Stephen? One leaving White River Junction at eight-thirty tonight. I can make that by car if I leave right away. (*Looks at his watch.*) Yes, I'm coming. At the Windsor Station then. One moment! What's the phone number of the hospital? Mount Royal, 9000. (JUDITH *writes down number.*) And your house, Stephen? Yes, I must! Somerset 2040. Right. Tomorrow morning, then. Good-bye. (*Hangs up.*)

JUDITH. I know, dear, but this is *your* job. (*Kissing him.*) I'll get your bag, darling. There's time to have tea before you go. (*Going off* L.) Miss Jenny, tea for Fred before he goes.

JENNY. (*Off stage.*) It's ready now, Mrs. Fred.

(JUDITH *exits.* STEELE *makes note from a time table. Sotto voce.*)

STEELE (*Reading time table.*) Nothing till two o'clock! (MISS JENNY *enters with teapot, crosses to* C. STEELE *hears her and starts.*) Oh, Miss Jenny, I'm just making a list of trains, phone numbers, and so forth. I'm leaving this here. I'm giving it to you, in case you need it.

JENNY. (*Hesitates* C.) I don't think I'll need it. (*She crosses to tea table—puts teapot down.*)

STEELE. One can never tell. (*Places it carefully on desk.*) I don't see why the devil Platt can't get someone in Montreal.

JENNY. (*Crosses to* C., *then over to desk.*) Now don't worry, Frederick!

STEELE. (MISS JENNY *crosses to him at desk.*) All right. But if anything goes wrong, of any kind, you're to phone me immediately. You can reach me at one or the other of those numbers. You'll take care of her?

(*Enter* JUDITH *with a bag.* MISS JENNY *exits above desk and* L.)

JUDITH. (*Puts case* L. *end of desk.*) Here are your things, Fred. (*Crosses back of him to* R.)

STEELE. Thanks, darling.

JUDITH. (*Crosses to sofa.*) Fred, dear, you must have tea before you go. You need it!

STEELE. Judith, dear —— (*Rises, does not finish sentence, but sits before tea table at sofa—*L. *end.*)

JUDITH. (*Sits* C. *in sofa.*) Hasn't it been a perfect day?

STEELE. (*Sits* L. *of her.*) Has it? Yes, of course it has.

JUDITH. (*Pouring.*) Strong, no sugar, no cream, no charm, bitter, repulsive. There. (*Hands it to him.*) Sandwiches?

STEELE. Thanks. (*Takes one.*)

JUDITH. (*Offering plate.*) Cake?

STEELE. No, thanks.

JUDITH. Remember Miss Jenny's feelings.

STEELE. Right.

JUDITH. I was going over the books today.

STEELE. What did you find?

JUDITH. Certain debts owing my husband that will never be paid.

STEELE. Not one that you haven't repaid a thousand times.

JUDITH. Have I really been a good wife?

STEELE. You!—you idiot!

JUDITH. Oh, I've loved it so—every minute. How can I make you understand? Look out there. (*Points to window* U. R.) Somehow it's been like that—shining and quiet.

STEELE. It's deep winter.

JUDITH. Deep winter. And behold—snow was upon the earth—and silence, and all things had been fulfilled that were to be, and there was no emptiness under heaven.

STEELE. (*Puts teacup down on table.*) Judith, dear, I—er—left a memorandum there. Don't lose it. You'll be able to reach me at any time.

JUDITH. I see.

STEELE. If anything—anything —— Oh, my God! Judith.

JUDITH. Shh, darling. I walked to the mill dam this morning!

STEELE. I haven't been there lately.

JUDITH. We'll go soon.

67

STEELE. The moment I'm back.

JUDITH. There's snow on the evergreens.

STEELE. Snow everywhere.

JUDITH. Evergreens are wiser than other trees. They stay awake all winter while the others sleep. (STEELE *smiles.*) Fred, I've found out at last.

STEELE. What?

JUDITH. What the hills do to you. I understand.

STEELE. You understand everything, dear.

JUDITH. Oh, darling, you must never leave them. You must go on living here, where you can see them. (*Rises, crosses to behind table* R.) The bulbs came this afternoon. I took the books to Mrs. Waring. I wrote Sears, Roebuck for the new door-scraper. Fred, you must go now.

STEELE. Yes—yes.

JUDITH. Here's your coat, dear —— (*Helps him into coat.*)

STEELE. Judith, I'm not going. I'll call—(*Crosses to desk, picks up phone.*)—Platt and tell him.

JUDITH. My darling. Come here.

STEELE. I thought I could. But I can't!!

JUDITH. Fred, remember our bargain. (*Takes phone from him.*)

STEELE. (*Releases phone.*) Yes. Words, just words! And I didn't know what they meant. God, to be given so much! This little time in all my life, and then to have it taken away. There's a limit to what a man can bear.

JUDITH. (*Very firm, very crisp.*) Fred, we have just one minute together. Look at me.—(*Hand out, he comes to her.*) I was never to fail you or keep you from your best.—We've had our love and we're complete, nothing can hurt us now; what we've had can never be wiped out. That's our victory—our victory over the dark. And it is a *real* victory because we're not afraid.

STEELE. (*Long pause as they look into each other's eyes. His tenseness relaxes and he smiles.*) Thank you, Judith.

JUDITH. And you'll never, never look back.

STEELE. Never.

JUDITH. Hold me close, darling.

STEELE. (*Holding her close.*) I'll hold you this way—forever.

JUDITH. Forever is now?—Isn't it?

STEELE. Yes. (*Kisses her. Then abruptly tears himself away. Takes coat and hat, putting them on as he walks to door* L. *Calls.*) I'm off, Miss Jenny! Take care of everything. (*Turns rapidly into room. Picks up bag. At door, he stops and turns briskly.*) Good luck!

JUDITH. (*Who has not moved.*) Good luck!

(STEELE *has gone. Door is closed. A moment later we hear roar of his car's engine.* JUDITH *has moved to window to see him go. She turns after a moment to see* MISS JENNY *in doorway,* L.)

JENNY. He's gone.

(JUDITH *closes door*—U. C.)

JUDITH. (*She takes up memorandum from desk, studies it, walks slowly to the fireplace. Stands facing flames, slowly she tears it across and throws the fragments in the blaze. Then she turns to* MISS JENNY.) Yes, Miss Jenny, he's gone, but not far.

CURTAIN

PROPERTY LIST

ACT I

A few books.
Typed pages for case history.
Shadow box—for X-ray—with wire and plug, and electric light.
Cigarettes.
Tray with a few surgical instruments.

Pencil flashlight.
Ophthalmoscope.
Small wooden cube.
Pencil.
Small piece of burlap.
Small piece of silk.
Wet X-ray plates.

ACT II

Telegram.
Tray with coffee things.
Cigarettes.
Judith's handbag.

Rabbit foot.
Tray with glasses, whiskey and soda.
Silver cup.

ACT III

Chemical tubes.
A few small bottles.
Instrument sterilizer.
A few instruments.
Tray with milk and sandwiches.
Tray with tea things, plates, etc.
Plate with cake.
Cushion.
Pipe and tobacco pouch.
Appointment book.
Ledger and a few bills.
Time table.
Memo pad and pencil.

Two or three books.
Large parcel post package, with smaller packages inside.
Plant bulbs.
Ivy, etc., in two or three pots.
Postman's small receipt book and pencil.
Letters.
Log for fire.
Suitcase for Steele.
Suitcase for Judith.
Whiskey and glass.

NEW
PLAYS

THE LIGHTS
by Howard Korder

THE TRIUMPH OF LOVE
by James Magruder

LATER LIFE
by A.R. Gurney

THE LOMAN FAMILY PICNIC
by Donald Margulies

A PERFECT GANESH
by Terrence McNally

SPAIN
by Romulus Linney

Write for information as to
availability
DRAMATISTS PLAY SERVICE, Inc.
440 Park Avenue South   New York, N.Y. 10016

NEW
PLAYS

LONELY PLANET
by Steven Dietz

THE AMERICA PLAY
by Suzan-Lori Parks

THE FOURTH WALL
by A.R. Gurney

JULIE JOHNSON
by Wendy Hammond

FOUR DOGS AND A BONE
by John Patrick Shanley

DESDEMONA, A PLAY ABOUT A
HANDKERCHIEF
by Paula Vogel

Write for information as to
availability
DRAMATISTS PLAY SERVICE, Inc.
440 Park Avenue South   New York, N.Y. 10016